THE
KINGFISHER
FACTS
AND
RECORDS
BOOK

Deputy Art Director	Mike Buckley
Art Editor	Keith Davis
Designer	Joe Conneally
Editors	Fergus Collins, Jonathan Stroud
Editorial Assistant	Robert Cave
Editorial Coordinator	Denise Heal
Picture Researcher	Tara McCormack
DTP Coordinator	Nicky Studdart
Production Controller	Jacquie Horner
Artwork Archivists	Wendy Allison, Steve Robinson
Indexer	Sue Lightfoot

KINGFISHER
Larousse Kingfisher Chambers Inc.
95 Madison Avenue
New York, New York 10016

Produced by Scintilla Editorial
33 Great Portland Street
London WIN 5DD

First published in 2000
1 3 5 7 9 10 8 6 4 2
1TR/0400/TWP/HBM(MNA)/150ARM

LIBRARY OF CONGRESS CATALOGING-IN-PUBLICATION DATA
has been applied for.

ISBN 0-7534-5270-7

Printed in Singapore

THE KINGFISHER FACTS AND RECORDS BOOK

KINGFISHER

NEW YORK

INTRODUCTION

Welcome to *The Kingfisher Facts and Records Book*. In the following pages you will find an abundance of intriguing information about a staggering variety of subjects. Divided into 11 fact-filled sections, there are exciting insights into everything from space to movies and nature to art.

The Kingfisher Facts and Records Book is an exploration and celebration of our incredible world and the achievements of its many remarkable people. As well as examining earth and its natural wonders, the book highlights key discoveries, crucial moments in history, and great human feats.

Discover who made the first space explorations; which pop artist sold the most albums; how many times we breathe in our lives; which is the world's tallest building; where soccer comes from; which is the oldest tree . . . and many more.

INVENTIONS!
Learn about amazing inventions, such as this early submarine. It was used by the United States against Britain during the Revolutionary War (1775–80).

RICHES!
Discover the most precious objects on earth, such as the British Crown Jewels. Read about the largest diamond ever discovered and the most expensive bottle of wine!

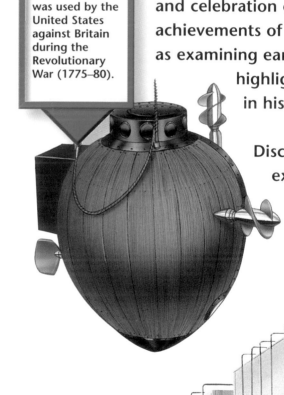

BIZARRE FACTS!
Did you know that in Australia trucks with several trailers are used instead of trains for transporting freight?

SOLAR SYSTEM

The solar system is made up of the sun and its nine orbiting planets. The sun exerts a huge gravitational pull on the planets, preventing them from drifting away.

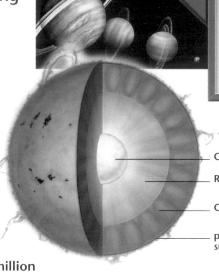

FACTS AND FIGURES

The sun is so huge that it comprises 99.8 percent of the solar system's total mass.

Jupiter has the shortest day of any of the planets, lasting just under 10 hours.

Aristarchus, in 270 B.C., was the first to propose that the earth revolves around the sun.

Venus is the closest planet to earth. It is a mere 26 million miles away.

The volcano Olympus Mons on Mars is 75,000 ft. high. Mt. Everest is only 29,000 ft. high.

Mariner 2 was the first space probe to visit another planet. It reached Venus in 1962.

The Sun

The sun is actually a small star. It is 30,000 times heavier than earth and has a diameter of nearly 1 million miles. Nuclear reactions at its core produce immense heat and light. The temperature is 59 million°F at the core, but only 10,000°F on the surface—still 24 times as hot as a typical oven. It uses 4–7 million tons of fuel a second, yet is so huge that all the fuel it has ever used equals only 0.01 percent of its original weight when it began shining 5 billion years ago.

Core

Radiative zone

Convective zone

photosphere—the sun's surface

The Planets

Venus takes longer to spin on its axis than to orbit the sun—so its days are longer than its years.

The nine planets range in size from tiny Pluto, which is smaller than earth's moon, to Jupiter, which has a diameter 11 times greater than earth. Mercury, Venus, Earth, and Mars, the inner planets, are small, rocky worlds. Jupiter, Saturn, Uranus, and Neptune are huge and consist of gas, liquid, and ice. Little is known about cold and remote Pluto at the outer edge of the solar system. Some scientists believe that there is a tenth planet beyond Pluto still to be discovered—Planet X.

CHARON
Pluto is twice the size of its moon, Charon. Pluto was located in 1930, but Charon was only discovered in 1978.

MERCURY
Distance from sun: 43.4 million miles
Diameter: 3,024 mi.
Day: 58 days 14 hrs
Year: 88 days

VENUS
Distance from sun: 67.7 million miles
Diameter: 7,509 mi.
Day: 244 days
Year: 225 days

EARTH
Distance from sun: 94.5 million miles
Diameter: 7,908 mi.
Day: 24 hrs
Year: 365 days

Measurements in earth days and years. Distance from the sun is average.

VOYAGER I & II
Launched in 1979, two identical probes were used to explore Saturn. *Voyager II* continued to the outer planets.

GAS GIANT
Saturn is made up of swirling gases, including hydrogen and helium. Its 23 moons, however, are mostly rocky.

RINGS
Saturn's rings are not solid, but are made up of billions of pieces of rocky debris that orbit the planet.

Probing the Planets

Little would be known about the planets without space probes. These crewless craft, such as *Pioneer,* have visited every planet except Pluto. In 1997, NASA's *Pathfinder* landed on Mars. It carried a remote controlled vehicle, which scientists on earth used to examine the planet's surface. The probe *Voyager 1,* launched in 1977, visited Jupiter and Saturn. It has now left the solar system and in 1998 was over 6 billion miles from earth—the remotest engineered object ever. Probes are today's great explorers of the unknown and each year they reveal more about the mysteries of space.

Until the 1500s, most people thought that the sun and its planets revolved around the earth.

DATABANK

Q What is the difference between the length of a planet's day and its year?

A A day is the time a planet takes to rotate once. A year is how long it takes to orbit the sun.

Q What is the huge red spot that can be seen regularly passing across the surface of Jupiter?

A It is a storm 24,800 miles in diameter that has been raging for at least 300 years.

MARS
Distance from sun: 154.9 million miles
Diameter: 4,212 mi.
Day: 24.5 hrs
Year: 687 days

JUPITER
Distance from sun: 507.1 million miles
Diameter: 88,536 mi.
Day: 9 hrs 55 mins
Year: 11 years, 314 days

SATURN
Distance from sun: 936.2 million miles
Diameter: 74,400 mi.
Day: 10 hrs 40 mins
Year: 29 years, 168 days

URANUS
Distance from sun: 1,867 million miles
Diameter: 31,620 mi.
Day: 17 hrs 15 mins
Year: 84 years, 4 days

NEPTUNE
Distance from sun: 2,822 million miles
Diameter: 30,690 mi.
Day: 16 hrs 7 mins
Year: 164 years, 298 days

PLUTO
Distance from sun: 4,587 million miles
Diameter: 1,426 mi.
Day: 6 days 9 hrs
Year: 247 years, 256 days

DEEPER SPACE

Little is known about deepest space. Scientists are eager to find out more about galaxies, stars, and black holes so that they can develop a better understanding of the universe, earth, and the origins of life itself.

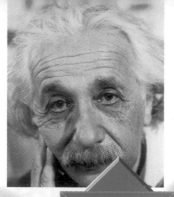

EINSTEIN
Albert Einstein's general theory of relativity, published in 1915, shows how time and space are linked. It provides the framework for our modern ideas about the universe.

 ## Big Bang

There are many ideas about how the universe was created, but most scientists now think it started with the "Big Bang." They believe the universe once fitted into a tiny ball the size of a pinhead. This ball exploded and released all the matter that now makes up the universe. Scientists still argue about how the universe may end. Some believe it will go on expanding forever, others think it could reach a point—billion of years from now—when it starts to contract into a tiny ball again.

A light year is the distance that light travels in a year. Light travels about 186,282 miles per second.

Our solar system is 12 light hours—not light years—wide, so it is small compared to a galaxy.

SCORCHER
After the Big Bang, it took over 300,000 years for the universe to cool enough for the first atoms to form.

EXPANDING UNIVERSE
Galaxies began to form 1.4 million years after the Big Bang. The universe is still expanding 12 billion years later.

DEEP FIELD SCAN
In 1995, the Hubble Space Telescope spotted 1,500 galaxies during a 10-day scan of a single stretch of sky.

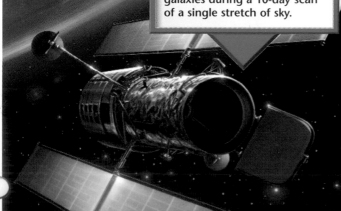

DATABANK

INPUT	OUTPUT
Q How wide is the Milky Way?	**A** The main part of the Milky Way is 75,000 light years wide.
Q Do stars move in space?	**A** Yes, our solar system orbits the galaxy every 200 million years.
Q How does the Hubble Space Telescope work?	**A** As it is a crewless satellite, it radios its findings back to earth.
Q How hot is it at the center of a supernova?	**A** Some scientists estimate that it may be 9 billion°F.

Stars and Black Holes

Stars vary widely in size and brightness. Our sun is small compared to giant stars like Betelgeuse, which has a diameter 700 times larger. Stars are born in huge clouds of debris called nebulas. Here gravity eventually pulls the debris together so tightly that a nuclear reaction takes place, emitting light and heat—a star is born! When a star runs out of hydrogen at the end of its life, a number of things can happen. A star the size of our sun, or smaller, will eventually shrink and cool. Larger stars explode as supernovas, their remains forming a nebula. If the star is more than five times the size of our sun, the star's core could collapse upon itself to form a black hole.

Black holes are not really holes, but solid spherical bodies with amazing levels of gravity.

NO ESCAPE
The dark area at the center of a black hole is called the event horizon. Not even light can escape its grasp.

DRAINING AWAY
A nearby star is unable to prevent its material from being sucked away by the pull of the black hole's powerful gravity.

Galaxies

A galaxy contains millions of stars, bound together with gases and dust by their gravitational pull toward each other. The sun is just one of the 200 billion stars in our own galaxy, the Milky Way. The Milky Way resembles a spiral-shaped disk with a bright, bulging cloud at its center. This cloud is so bright that we cannot see what lies at its center, but some scientists believe that it could be hiding a black hole. There are uncounted millions of galaxies in the universe and they take many different shapes. Some resemble spirals or balls, others are more irregular, resembling misty clouds. In 1937, Clyde Tombaugh, who also located the planet Pluto, discovered that galaxies, like stars, are arranged into clusters.

A pulsar is a rapidly rotating star that spins faster than a washing machine—up to 622 times a second.

FACTS AND FIGURES

The nearest galaxy to our own is Magellan, which is over 150,000 light years away.

700 baby stars have been seen in the Orion Nebula, a cloud of matter where stars form.

Proxima Centauri is the nearest star to our sun. It is 25 trillion miles away.

The earth is roughly 30,000 light years away from the center of the Milky Way.

The Crab Nebula is the remnant of a supernova that the Chinese saw in A.D. 1054.

STAR SPIRAL
At 2,200,000 light years from earth, the Andromeda spiral galaxy may contain as many as 400 billion stars.

PEOPLE IN SPACE

Even before the 1900s, people dreamed of traveling beyond the earth's atmosphere and exploring space. But it was not until rocket technology was developed during World War II (1939–45) that such fantasies could be turned into reality.

 ## The Space Race

In the 1950s, 60s, and 70s, the Soviet Union and the United States were the only countries wealthy enough to build space rockets. However, because of differing political beliefs, the two countries did not trust each other. Instead of cooperating, they competed fiercely. The Soviets led the way by sending the first satellite into space in 1957. In the same year, they also sent the first animal into orbit—a dog named Laika on board the spacecraft *Sputnik 2*. On April 12, 1961, the Soviet cosmonaut Yuri Gagarin made history in *Vostok I* by becoming the first person in space. After orbiting the earth once, he made a safe landing back on earth. In 1962, John Glenn became the first American to reach orbit. After several more space flights, the Soviet Union and the U.S. turned their attention to the greatest goal of all—the moon.

YURI GAGARIN
Having survived his epic trip into space, Gagarin became a global hero. He was killed in a plane crash in 1968.

From 1959 to 1976 there were 48 Soviet and 31 American crewless moon missions. About half failed.

There is no wind or atmosphere on the moon. Astronauts' footprints will remain unchanged forever.

SATURN V
Used on moon missions, this huge rocket was 360 ft. tall—the same height as a twenty-five story building.

DATABANK

INPUT	OUTPUT
Q How many people have walked on the moon's surface?	**A** 12, all American. The Soviets abandoned crewed moon flights.
Q How long would it take to travel by space rocket to Mars?	**A** It would take up to a year to travel the 48.4 million miles to Mars.
Q Who was the first woman to be sent into space?	**A** The Soviet Valentina Tereshkova visited space in 1963.
Q Why did the Space Shuttle *Challenger* explode in 1986?	**A** Frost before take off weakened seals on the fuel tank.

THE FUTURE
Some asteroids are made of metals, such as iron. Eventually it may be possible to drag them into earth's orbit to be mined.

SPACE POWER
One day, solar power collectors may be able to beam the sun's energy to earth to generate electricity.

Giant Leap

The U.S. was determined to be the first to put a person on the moon. In 1969, after a series of test flights, the Saturn V rocket *Apollo 11* set out on this ultimate mission. On July 20, while the command module orbited the moon, the landing craft, called *Eagle*, detached itself with Buzz Aldrin and Neil Armstrong inside. After a risky descent, *Eagle* landed on a flat plain. Finally, in front of a television audience of millions, Armstrong, followed by Aldrin, stepped out of the *Eagle* to explore the alien landscape. The landing was a triumph for NASA and prompted worldwide celebrations.

MOON BUGGY
Made from light aluminum, the lunar rover was used to explore large areas of the moon's rocky surface.

Despite several fatal accidents in earth's atmosphere, no astronauts have yet been killed in space.

FACTS AND FIGURES

Rockets have to travel at a speed of 7 miles/sec. to pull clear of the earth's gravity.

The longest stay in space is 437 days 18 hours by the Soviet Valeri Polyakov.

The first space walk was performed by Aleksey Leonov in 1965.

In 1998, John Glenn, aged 77, became the oldest man to visit space.

The Apollo program returned 663 lbs. of moon rock to the earth.

The first docking between U.S. and Soviet spacecraft occurred in 1975.

 # Space Stations

While the U.S. missions to the moon continued in the early 1970s, the Soviets built space stations to be used as orbiting laboratories. The first of these were the Salyuts but they were replaced by the *Mir* in 1986. This was still in use in the late 1990s. The U.S. responded with the *Skylab* space station in 1974 and later with the space shuttle, which has since been used to put satellites into orbit and conduct experiments in space. In the 1990s, the U.S. and Russia began cooperating on the international space station *Freedom*, which will be completed soon after the year 2000. There are also plans to revisit the moon and build a permanent base there.

The space shuttle is a reusable spacecraft. The first shuttle, *Columbia*, took off in 1981.

SKY WATCHING

The night sky has long been a source of wonder. Some people saw images of gods in the stars, while others used the night sky to predict the future—but all have felt a sense of awe.

 ## Astronomers

People have probably studied the stars since prehistoric times, but it was in 2000 B.C. that the ancient Babylonians began to name groups, or constellations, of stars. Later, the Chinese and Egyptians used the stars to develop calendars that could predict the changing seasons. Astronomy was revolutionized in 1609, when Galileo Galilei adapted the newly invented telescope for sky watching. He made detailed observations of the moon and discovered some of Jupiter's moons. Astronomers used telescopes to map the night sky and, later, split their maps into two to compare the night skies in the Northern and Southern hemispheres.

Shooting stars are particles of dust that burn up brightly as they enter earth's atmosphere.

ASTRONOMER
Ptolemy, an Egyptian (A.D. 90–168), used Babylonian star charts to explain his theories of the universe.

SPACE CRATER
50,000 years ago a meteorite landed in Arizona, leaving a crater .14 miles wide.

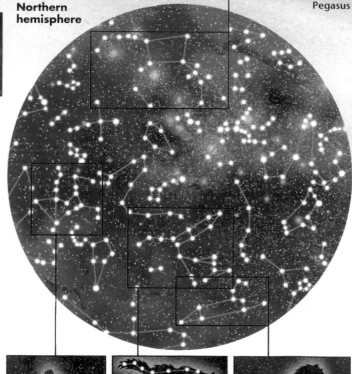

Pegasus

Southern hemisphere

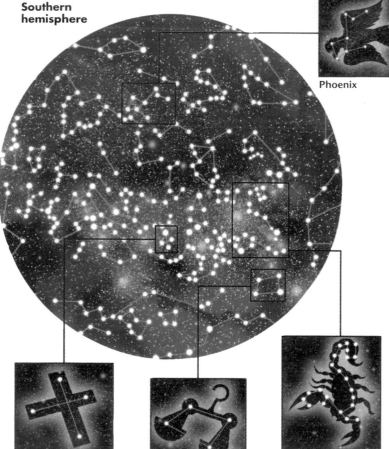

Northern hemisphere

Phoenix

The Southern Cross

Libra, the scales

Scorpius, the scorpion

Hercules

Ursa Major, the great bear

Leo, the lion

MAPS OF THE STARS
Stars seen from earth are grouped into constellations. People in the south have a different star map to those in the north.

FACTS AND FIGURES

Halley's Comet was discovered by Edmund Halley in 1682. It orbits earth every 76 years.

The brightest star in the night sky is Sirius, sometimes known as the dog star.

The most frequently seen comet is called Encke. It orbits earth every three years.

Tycho Brahe (1546–1601) charted 777 stars using his unaided eyes.

Keck Telescopes I and II are the largest on earth, with apertures of 35.6 ft.

The Great Comet of 1863 had the longest tail recorded, stretching 496 million miles.

COMET'S ICY CORE
The head of a comet is only a few miles wide but its tail of vaporized ice may be millions of miles long.

Comets

A comet is a lump of ice in orbit around the sun. Its characteristic tail forms as it melts with the sun's heat. In the past, people thought that comets were omens of good or evil. Halley's Comet appears in the Bayeux tapestry as a warning of William the Conqueror's victory at the Battle of Hastings in England in 1066. Today, scientists believe that comets come from the Oort Cloud, a cluster of billions of objects outside the orbit of the planet Pluto.

William Herschel was the first man to discover a planet by telescope when he located Uranus in 1781.

Solar Eclipses

At least twice a year, the moon's orbit places it between the earth and the sun, preventing some sunlight from reaching us. This event is called a solar eclipse and can be seen in one of three ways. A partial eclipse occurs when only part of the moon's shadow, or penumbra, is seen from earth. An annular eclipse occurs when the moon is at its farthest point from earth and does not appear big enough to cover the sun. A total eclipse occurs when the moon entirely covers the sun. Those directly beneath the eclipse on earth experience a period of almost "nighttime" darkness in the middle of the day.

During a total eclipse, the wind drops and animals become eerily quiet in anticipation of nightfall.

DATABANK

Q What causes the strange lights in the sky known as the *Aurora Borealis* and *Aurora Australis*?

A These lights are caused by the sun's radiation striking earth's atmosphere at the two poles.

Q What's the difference between an asteroid and a meteor?

A An asteroid is a rock that orbits the sun. A meteor is a rock that enters earth's atmosphere.

IN THE MOON'S SHADOW
In a total eclipse, the darkest area, or umbra, is only 93 miles wide and sweeps across the earth's surface as it rotates.

VIOLENT EARTH

Earth is the only planet in our solar system capable of sustaining life, yet it is still a volatile place. Volcanoes burst through its delicate crust and earthquakes regularly shake the land.

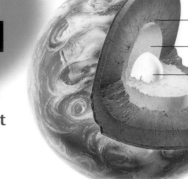

- Crust: 3-22 mi. thick
- Mantle: 1,800 mi. thick
- Outer core: 1,360 mi. thick
- Inner core: 740 mi. thick

 ## Fragile Crust

Earth's crust is only 3 miles thick in places and is divided into pieces, known as tectonic plates. Molten rock swirls beneath the crust, reaching 11,400°F at the earth's core. Under pressure, the rock forces itself through weaknesses in the crust, particularly along the edges of the plates. The movement of molten rock causes the plates to crash together or drift apart, causing volcanoes and earthquakes. Two areas famous for plate activity are the Rift Valley in Africa and the San Andreas Fault in North America.

Continental plates move at the same rate that fingernails grow—about 2-4 inches a year.

WAFER THIN
The earth's crust is incredibly thin compared to the immensely thick layers of molten rock beneath it—like the outer skin of an onion compared to the rest of the vegetable.

Shaken and Stirred

As tectonic plates grind against each other, enormous pressure builds up until the ground suddenly buckles, causing an earthquake. Waves of energy flow through the ground and can flatten entire cities. Scientists measure these "seismic" waves on the Richter scale as a number from zero to 10. A powerful earthquake that occurred in Alaska in 1964 measured 9.2 on the Richter scale. It caused few deaths because the area was sparsely populated. Earthquakes beneath the sea can create huge waves, called tsunamis. Reaching heights of 160 feet and speeds of 560 miles per hour, these walls of water cannot be stopped. In 1896, in Honshu, Japan, 26,000 people were killed by a tsunami.

FACTS AND FIGURES

The 1883 eruption of Krakatau in Indonesia was heard 1,364 miles away.

The Krakatau eruption also created a tsunami 115 ft. high, ravaging nearby coasts.

The longest earthquake on record occurred in Alaska in 1964. It lasted four minutes.

90,000 people are thought to have been killed by the Tambora volcano in Indonesia in 1815.

The earthquake in Kobe, Japan, in 1995, caused over $100 billion worth of damage.

The world's tallest volcano is Aconcagua in Argentina. It is 22,800 ft. high.

The 1976 earthquake in Tangshan, China killed over 240,000 people.

Volcanic activity that began at Kilauea, Hawaii in 1790 has continued ever since.

ALL SHOOK UP
The Mercalli Scale measures an earthquake's damage. It ranges from I (gentle tremor) to XII (total destruction).

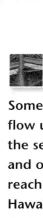

Volcanoes

Some volcanoes ooze rivers of molten lava that flow up to 3 miles per hour. When these occur on the seabed, the lava cools and hardens in the water and other layers pile up on top. These eventually reach such a height that an island is created. The Hawaiian islands were formed this way, as was Surtsey, which appeared off the coast of Iceland in 1963. Other eruptions, such as Tambora in 1815 and Krakatau in 1883, are much more violent. Pressure builds up causing explosions, which eject ash, showers of rocks, and poisonous gases.

The Krakatau eruption created a gigantic tsunami that carried a ship 1.6 miles up a river.

HOT STUFF
When Mt. Pelee erupted in 1902, hot gas and ash destroyed the port of St. Pierre in Martinique, West Indies.

PRIMEVAL FORCE
In 1980, Mt. St. Helens in Washington erupted violently, destroying 250 homes and killing 57 people.

BLAST FROM THE PAST
In A.D. 79, Mt. Vesuvius in Italy, suddenly erupted, covering Pompeii in ash. The people had little chance of escaping.

DOOM RIVER
Liquid lava from a volcano is around 1800°F, hot enough to burn anything in its way. It can also travel at great speed. As it cools, lava hardens into solid rock and turns black.

LAND AND SEA

Earth is a planet of great contrasts. Most of its surface is covered with vast oceans that teem with life, yet large tracts of land are barren deserts. To cap it all, the two poles are frozen, inhospitable wildernesses.

 ## Oceans

About 71 percent of the earth's surface is covered with water and 97 percent of this is found in the oceans. Close to land the water is shallow, and abundant with life. The majority of marine life is found here. Farther out, oceans can be very deep. The Marianas Trench in the Pacific Ocean descends 36,200 feet below sea level—the deepest water on earth. The water pressure at the seabed is too great for humans to survive without specially adapted submarines, so most of the ocean floor remains unexplored.

Tides are caused by the gravitational pull of the sun and moon on the seas and oceans.

OCEAN BLUE
The Atlantic Ocean (top) is 41 million square miles. It is small compared to the Pacific Ocean (above). This covers 70 million square miles and could fit all the world's land within it.

SEABED
Plants, such as seaweed, survive only in shallow coastal areas where sunlight penetrates to the seabed.

Shallow waters close to land support many plants, fish, and other creatures.

Midocean ridges are undersea mountain ranges.

The average depth of the oceans is 11,500 ft.

Deep ocean trenches are home to strange fish, mollusks, and crustaceans.

Volcanoes under the sea sometimes build up to form islands.

JUST ABOUT BEAR-ABLE
Many animals, big and small, visit the Arctic in summer to feed. In winter, they travel to warmer areas farther south.

Icy Wastes

Nowhere on earth is as cold and barren as the North and South poles. The Arctic, in the north, is a frozen ocean; the Antarctic, in the south, is a huge continent, 98 percent of which is covered in ice up to 13,000 feet thick. It is the coldest place on earth with average winter temperatures of –76°F, so few animals live there. The Arctic is warmer, reaching –40°F in winter. In summer, large parts of the polar ice sheet break off, forming icebergs.

EVEREST
The world's tallest mountain soars 29,000 ft. above sea level. It has claimed the lives of many climbers.

VERTICAL VISTA
The Grand Canyon is the world's largest gorge. Its steep walls were carved out by the Colorado River flowing through it.

High and Low

A mountain range is formed when huge rocks are forced upward as a result of a collision between sections of the earth's crust known as plates. The highest mountain range, the Himalayas, is growing taller every year as the Indian plate pushes into the Asian plate. The world's longest mountain chain is the Andes, which runs for 4,500 miles through South America. Even as mountains rise, the forces of erosion, such as wind and water, are wearing them down. Over time, water and ice flowing down the mountainsides carve out valleys.

The top of the valley is eroded into a circular shape.

The glacier picks up rock debris as it moves.

 # Just Deserts

Deserts are dry areas with little rainfall or plant life. They cover a third of the world's land and include the Kalahari Desert in southern Africa and the Arabian Desert in the Middle East. The largest desert is the Sahara, in Africa, which covers 4 million square miles. In the hottest months of the year, the temperature can reach highs of 136°F. Saharan animals are specially adapted to survive this heat.

Although it is covered in ice, the Antarctic is a desert because little rain falls and the air is very dry.

GLACIER
A glacier is a huge body of ice that slowly slides down a mountainside, gouging out a U-shaped valley as it does so. Glaciers move very slowly—by only a few feet a year.

FACTS AND FIGURES

The coldest temperature ever recorded on earth was –128.2°F, logged in Antarctica in 1983.

Lambert Glacier, in the Antarctic, is the world's largest—434 miles long.

Mont Blanc is the tallest mountain in Europe. It is just over half the size of Mt. Everest.

ENVIRONMENT

The environment is the world around us, including the land, sea, and air and all the plants and animals that share the planet. Everything exists together in a delicate balance. The actions of humans are starting to affect this balance, with potentially devastating consequences for the future.

FORESTS
Over 14 percent of Brazil's rain forest (equal to an area the size of France) has been cut down to provide grazing land for cattle and wood for industry. This destruction is increasing.

 ## Climate: A Warmer World

The term "climate" refers to a region's typical weather: hot and dry, or cold and rainy, for instance. Weather is determined by the region's distance from the equator and the prevailing winds, but even the oceans and forests have an effect. Records show that earth's overall climate has been getting warmer since the 1600s, when the industrial age began. This "global warming" increases the risk of severe weather conditions, such as floods, drought, and hurricanes.

Global warming is melting the ice caps at the two poles and raising the level of the world's oceans.

 ## Greenhouse Effect

Earth is surrounded by a layer of gases—the atmosphere. This acts like a greenhouse, letting sunlight in, and stopping some of the sun's heat from escaping back into space. It keeps the earth warm enough for life. Most of the gas is carbon dioxide (CO_2), which is produced by animals and by burning fossil fuels, such as coal and oil. Today, scientists are worried that we produce too much CO_2, which adds to global warming.

OZONE HOLE
The ozone layer, which keeps out cancer-causing solar rays, is being destroyed by gases from some spray cans.

FACTS AND FIGURES

Wood pulp, for making paper and building materials, uses up four billion trees a year.

Worldwide, over 15,000 species of plants and animals are at risk of extinction.

In 1984, 2,500 people died after toxic gas leaked from a factory in Bhopal, India.

The U.S. is the biggest user of paper in the world— 67 million tons each year.

KILLER RAIN
Many trees are killed by acid rain, which forms when gases from cars and power stations mix with water in the clouds.

Living Planet

In 1979, U.K. scientist James Lovelock proposed the Gaia theory. He claimed that earth's living matter, air, oceans, and land interact with each other to keep the planet a fit place for life. Trees are an example of this. They take in water from the soil and release it from their leaves, where it then forms clouds and falls as rain. Trees also absorb the waste gas carbon dioxide (CO_2) from the air and release oxygen, which every animal needs in order to live. Humans disrupt this delicate process. Clearing rain forests limits the number of trees, so CO_2 builds up and increases global warming. Fewer trees also means less rainfall, so areas of fertile land can become dry, hostile desert.

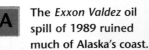

In some parts of the world, huge windmills harness the power of the wind to produce electricity.

OIL SPILLS
Every year, leaks from oil tankers and pipelines kill thousands of seabirds and other forms of marine life. Major oil spills can devastate coastal habitats and important fishing grounds.

A Greener Future

Governments worldwide are taking steps to protect the environment. We can all help by becoming energy efficient: insulating our homes, for example, means less energy is wasted. Instead of burning fossil fuels, more of our energy needs could be met by using non-polluting forms, such as solar, wind, and wave power. Recycling paper, cans, wood, and plastic, preserves natural resources. Trees can be planted to replace those that are lost, and we can help protect wildlife habitats.

SOLAR ENERGY
One day, cars may be fuelled by energy from solar panels, which make electricity from sunlight—without pollution.

DATABANK

INPUT

Q Which oil spill has had the worst effect on the environment?

Q Which U.S. city has the poorest air quality?

Q Where was the world's worst air pollution disaster?

Q Which European country has suffered most from acid rain?

OUTPUT

A The *Exxon Valdez* oil spill of 1989 ruined much of Alaska's coast.

A San Bernardino, CA, had poor air quality for 106 days in 1997.

A In Indonesia, in 1997. Forest-burning caused record levels of smog.

A Over 51 percent of German forests have been damaged.

FOREST LOSS
In the clouds, pollution gases are turned into sulphuric and nitric acid. This falls as rain, polluting lakes and destroying huge areas of forest in Europe and North America.

WEATHER

Come sunshine, snow, wind, or rain, the weather affects every day of our lives. In some parts of the world, severe weather is a regular threat to life.

CHARTS
Lines of triangles on weather maps indicate cold air. Lines of semi-circles indicate warm air. They are called fronts.

 ## Forecasting

Weather forecasting is vital. Ships' captains need to know when it is safe to sail, for instance, and farmers must be told when tender crops need protection. Weather is determined by many factors, including humidity, temperature, and wind, which makes it very difficult to predict. Before the 1900s, forecasting mostly relied on folklore, but it has now become a science. Thousands of measurements are taken from weather stations on the ground and from satellites in space in order to spot changes in the weather. Even so, forecasts are not always accurate.

Roy Sullivan from Virginia was struck by lightning seven times.

TWISTER
A tornado is like a concentrated hurricane, only about 1,300 ft.-wide. It appears with little warning and causes much damage. The winds of a tornado can reach 280 mph.

 ## Raining Again...

A cloud is a vast accumulation of water droplets, drawn up as vapor from plants, rivers, and oceans. As water builds up in the cloud, the droplets grow until they are too heavy to stay up in the sky, so they fall as rain. The rainy season in Southeast Asia is called the monsoon. In some areas, such as Bangladesh and parts of China, this heavy, sustained downpour often floods huge areas of low-lying land, drowning many people. Rain may be accompanied by a thunderstorm. This is caused by a huge buildup of electricity in the rain clouds, which is released as a series of high-voltage flashes, seen as lightning. Because sound travels slower than light, the noise of these flashes, or thunder, is heard seconds later.

SKY-HIGH VOLTAGE
When a flash of lightning strikes the ground, a return stroke is sent back from the ground to the cloud instantly.

BLOW ME DOWN
Tornadoes are unpredictable. The funnel of air suddenly touches the ground without warning, destroying homes.

FACTS AND FIGURES

In 1989, a tornado that hit Shaturia, Bangladesh, left 1,300 dead and 50,000 homeless.

A typhoon that struck Hong Kong in 1906 may have killed as many as 10,000 people.

The world's worst hailstorm occurred in India in 1988 and killed 246 people.

An icestorm in Canada and the U.S. in 1998 caused $650 million worth of damage.

In 1998, Hurricane Mitch was responsible for over 10,000 deaths in Central America.

A cluster of tornadoes in the U.S. in 1985 killed 271 and caused $400 million damage.

More than 45,000 people were trapped by avalanches in the Alps in January 1951.

UP AND AWAY
Tornadoes are common in central and southeastern U.S. Some are strong enough to suck up large objects, such as cars. A freezer was once carried over a mile by a tornado.

FOREST FIRE
Drought turns forests into dry kindling. A spark can lead to fires causing millions of dollars' worth of damage.

 # Heat and Dust

In hot countries, the sun is the greatest killer. Drought occurs when the rains do not come. Without water, crops fail, animals die of thirst, and people starve. Africa is prone to drought, and in the mid-1980s millions in Ethiopia and Sudan starved. In both cases it took a major international aid program to stave off complete disaster. In the 1930s, severe drought in the Great Plains turned large stretches of farmland to dust, which simply blew away in the wind. The area became known as the "Dust Bowl."

The Sahara Desert is growing by up to 62 miles every year—partly because of drought.

 # When the Wind Blows

"Hurricane," "typhoon," and "cyclone" are different names for the same force of nature. It is a circular, rotating storm that forms at sea and may be to up to 372 miles across. With winds reaching 186 miles per hour, it can devastate coastal regions. Cyclones are found in the Indian Ocean, typhoons occur in the western Pacific, while hurricanes rip though the Caribbean and the southern coasts of the U.S. The winds and heavy rain sink ships, destroy houses and cause flooding. A hurricane that struck Texas in 1900 killed 8,000 people.

Hurricanes are usually given names, including Juan, in 1985; Andrew, in 1992; and Floyd, in 1999.

FLOOD TIDE
A cyclone that hit Bangladesh in 1991 killed up to 200,000 people, mainly in floods caused by rain and high seas.

PLANTS

Plants are crucial for life. They provide most of the oxygen that animals and humans breathe— and much of the food we eat.

GIANTS
Redwoods are the largest trees in the world. One specimen measured 368 ft. high. These enormous trees take 400 to 500 years to mature and live for up to 1,500 years.

RINGING THE CHANGES
Each year a tree produces a new layer or ring of wood. A dead tree's age can be calculated by counting the rings.

Plant

From tiny algae to gigantic trees, plants are everywhere. Some, like roses, have colorful flowers, while others, like mosses, seem dull—but each species fits into its environment. Unlike animals, plants cannot move to find food, so they must make their own using a process called photosynthesis. Plants contain a substance called chlorophyll—usually found in the leaves—which absorbs sunlight. This, mixed with minerals and water drawn from the soil by the roots, creates the energy plants need to grow.

Some plants rely on the wind to carry their pollen to another plant.

HOTLIPS PLANT
The bright, lipstick-red leaves of the hotlips plant are designed to attract insects to its tiny yellow flower.

Flowers

Plants evolved 550 million years ago, yet the first flowers appeared only 420 million years later. Plants that have flowers use them to reproduce. Bright flowers, such as cherry blossoms, contain sugary nectar that attracts insects, especially bees. As a bee feeds, pollen from the male part of the flower is rubbed onto the insect's body. If the bee then feeds on another cherry blossom, some pollen is rubbed off onto the female part of the flower, fertilizing it so that it can produce seeds and fruit.

SKUNK CABBAGE
This plant stinks of a skunk to attract flies. They crawl inside to lay eggs and pick up pollen on the way.

FACTS AND FIGURES

Scientists believe there are over 400,000 species of plants worldwide.

Rafflesia arnoldii is the largest flower in the world. Found in southeast Asia, it smells of rotten flesh!

Pacific giant kelp, a type of seaweed, grows up to 11 in. per day, creating underwater forests.

Pads of the Amazon water lily grow to 7 ft. wide and can support the weight of a child.

The coco de mer palm, found in the Seychelles, has the largest seeds in the world— they weigh up to 44 lbs.

A mature oak tree produces an average of 50,000 acorns each year.

 # Fungi

Fungi are not plants or animals. They do not have leaves and roots and they do not not make their own food. Instead, they feed on other animals and plants. Mushrooms are the visible fruits of the fungi. Most of a fungus' body consists of fine threads, which remain hidden underground or in the body of a dead tree or animal where they absorb nutrients. Although fungi such as field mushrooms, truffles, and morels are good to eat, many species, such as harmless-looking death caps, are deadly poisonous.

MUSHROOM
Poisonous mushrooms, including the fly agaric, figure in the folklore of many countries.

 # Predators

Some plants get vital minerals from an unusual source—animals. These plants have special leaves or hairs to trap and digest insects. Pitcher plants attract insects with their sweet scent and special tube-like leaves that collect rainwater. As a hungry insect climbs into the plant's tube, tiny hairs keep it from leaving. Eventually, the insect falls into the water and drowns. A fluid found in the leaves allows the plant to digest its meal.

Some plants, such as dodderplants and Indian pipes, gain all their food by living on other plants.

DATABANK

INPUT

Q How much of the world's land surface is covered with rain forest?

Q Why does a sycamore tree have a seed with a wing that "flies" like a helicopter?

Q Which is the world's longest-living tree and how long has it survived?

OUTPUT

A About 7 percent. However, it contains at least half of all animal species.

A The tree uses "flying" seeds to help them reach ground suitable for growing.

A In California, a bristlecone pine— named Methuselah— is 4,765 years old.

SWEET DRINK
Some plants are pollinated by species of bats and birds that feed on the nectar.

SNAP SHUT
If an insect lands in the open jaws of a Venus fly-trap, it touches tiny hairs, which close the trap in an instant.

PREHISTORIC ANIMALS

Animals lived on earth for billions of years before the first humans appeared. Early creatures were tiny, but later huge beasts appeared—from earthshaking dinosaurs to bizarre, ferocious mammals.

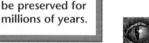

In the Beginning

Life, in the form of bacteria and algae, first appeared in the oceans some 3.5 billion years ago. However, the earliest fossils date from about 550 million years ago, and consist of simple sponges, worms, and trilobites. Now extinct, trilobites, which resembled large woodlice, were among the first animals to develop eyes. They were followed by creatures with shells, such as snails. Fish appeared about 500 million years ago. One species, *Dunkleosteus*, grew to 30 feet long—twice the size of a great white shark! By 400–300 million years ago, sea levels dropped and swamps became more common. Some fish developed legs, could breathe air, and were able to move around on land. These evolved into the first amphibians.

DIPLOCAULUS
Early amphibians were very strange looking. *Diplocaulus*, for example, had a boomerang-shaped head.

FOSSILS
Fossils, like this ammonite, form when animal bones or shells are covered with layers of sediment. Over time, these layers become solid rock. Fossils can be preserved for millions of years.

Dinosaurs

Amphibians were the earliest large land animals. However, they still relied heavily on water to survive and, with the rise of the reptiles, most became extinct. Reptiles evolved from amphibians but were better adapted to life on land. The largest and most successful reptiles were the "terrible lizards"— or dinosaurs. They ruled the earth for 180 million years. Most dinosaurs were plant eaters, and one of the largest of these was *Seismosaurus*, which was 164 feet long and weighed a titanic 90 tons. Like the antelopes of today, many dinosaurs lived in huge herds. They were preyed upon by gigantic predators, such as *Allosaurus* and *Tyrannosaurus*—the lions of their time. All dinosaurs died out suddenly 65 million years ago.

The first land creatures were the arthropods—forerunners of the insects of today.

Before the 1820s, dinosaur bones were thought to be those of dragons or even giant people.

HORNS OF A DILEMMA
Triceratops had huge horns on its head. These may have been used for defense against the terrifying *Tyrannosaurus rex*.

Up, Up, and Away

As the dinosaurs ruled the land, other reptiles took to the air. Known as pterosaurs, these creatures' leathery wings consisted of skin held outstretched by elongated finger bones. Although most species were small, *Quetzalcoatlus* and *Pteranodon* were the largest flying animals that have ever lived. The oldest known bird is the fully feathered *Archaeopteryx*, which is thought to have evolved from a tiny dinosaur. Today, some zoologists regard birds as modern-day dinosaurs. Reptiles also conquered the oceans. Some of these were huge. *Kronosaurus*, for example, had a skull 7 feet long—larger and more powerful than that of *Tyrannosaurus rex*! Other carnivorous sea reptiles, called ichthyosaurs—"fish lizards"— resembled a cross between a shark and a dolphin.

FLYING NIGHTMARE
Quetzalcoatlus is the largest flying reptile ever found. Its 39 ft. wingspan is equivalent to that of a small plane.

Elasmosaurus, a sea reptile, had a flexible neck 26 feet long. It was an expert at catching fish.

EARLY BIRD
Archaeopteryx was probably not a strong flier. It may have had to climb trees to gain enough height to fly or glide.

Early Mammals

Mammals existed as early as 200 million years ago, but they remained small until the dinosaurs became extinct. After this time, many mammals evolved to become as big as the reptiles they had replaced. *Indricotherium*, a relative of the rhino, was 26 feet long and weighed 30 tons—twice the size of the woolly mammoth, which was a giant ancestor of the modern elephant.

EARLY SHREW
Early mammals resembled shrews. They foraged only at night when the dinosaurs were inactive.

FACTS AND FIGURES

A flightless bird, *Diatryma*, was large enough to catch horses in its massive beak.

The first dinosaur to be discovered was *Megalosaurus*—named in the 1820s.

It is thought that 99.9 percent of all species that have ever existed are now extinct.

Tyrannosaurus' teeth were 5.8 in. long, about the size of a banana—but sharper!

The smallest known dinosaur was *Compsognathus*. It was about the size of a chicken.

DATABANK

Q Why did the dinosaurs become extinct?

A Many scientists believe that the dinosaurs died out after a huge meteorite struck earth.

Q Which animals did mammals evolve from?

A Mammals may have evolved from a group of mammal-like reptiles called cynodonts.

SMILER
The size of a lion, *Smilodon* may have preyed on animals as large as elephants. The elongated canine teeth might have been used to stab its victims to death.

INVERTEBRATES

Unlike fish, reptiles, and mammals, invertebrates have no backbone. From tiny mites to giant squid, invertebrates are some of the world's most amazing animals.

SOCIAL WORK
Leaf-cutter ants collect leaves for food for their colony. Each ant brings back a load heavier than itself.

AIRHOLES
As earthworms tunnel, they let oxygen into the soil. In areas that lack worms, soil quality is not as good.

Alien Lifeforms

Invertebrates often appear alien to us, so we fear them. For example, jellyfish have no eyes, while crabs, sponges, and worms lack recognizable heads. Yet some invertebrates are highly intelligent. Octopuses can unscrew lids of jars to get food and also learn new skills by watching other octopuses. The robber crab, a species that lives almost entirely on land, climbs palm trees to cut down coconuts. It then returns to the ground to feed.

THE STING
Jellyfish have soft bodies and tentacles armed with venomous stings. These are used to paralyze their prey.

The Great Barrier Reef in Australia is the largest structure made by animals—constructed entirely of coral.

FACTS AND FIGURES

The goliath bird-eating spider is the world's largest. Spread out, its legs span up to 10 in.

It is thought there may be 10 million species of insects still to be discovered.

A giant clam discovered off Japan's coast weighed 750 lbs.—the largest shellfish ever.

The cockroach is the fastest insect on land. It travels at about 4 mph.

The caterpillar of a *Polythemus* moth eats 86,000 times its birthweight before pupating.

Insects

Insects are the most common animals on earth, with about a million species, including butterflies, beetles, flies, wasps, and grasshoppers. Insects do not have internal skeletons like humans, but instead have a hard exterior, like a suit of armor. Some insects, like bees and ants, work together to find food and fight off enemies. Millions of ants live together in one nest serving a single queen. The queen ant's only job is to lay eggs.

BIG BEETLE
The heaviest insect is the goliath beetle. It grows as big as a man's fist and weighs up to 3.5 oz.

ATLAS MOTH
With a 9–11 in. wingspan, this moth is often mistaken for a bird. It has the largest antennae of any moth.

WOODY DISGUISE
Stick insects closely resemble the twigs they live on. One species is the longest of all insects, measuring over 19 in.

Arachnids

Scorpions and spiders are arachnids, and not insects. They are among the world's most feared animals. In some cases, this fear is justified. One species of Mexican scorpion kills more than 1,000 people a year, and it is claimed that the black widow spider's venom is 15 times more powerful than that of a rattlesnake. Many spiders spin a sticky web in order to catch food. The largest webs, at 5 feet in diameter, are those of the orb-weaving spider, which can catch small birds. Spider silk is the strongest of all natural or synthetic fibers. Scientists are trying to recreate it in laboratories so that it can be used by humans.

TAIL OF WOE
A scorpion has a sting in the end of its tail. This is mainly used in self-defense against animals that try to eat it.

Fishermen in Papua New Guinea use the huge webs of orb-weaving spiders as fishing nets.

Giants of the Deep

For centuries, stories of giant sea monsters were dismissed as myths. In 1887, however, the body of a giant squid was washed ashore on Cook Strait, New Zealand. It measured 62 feet from the tip of its tail to the end of its tentacles. Since then, more bodies have been found, but few people have ever seen a live specimen. The world's largest invertebrates, giant squid, remain a great mystery to science as they glide through the ocean depths.

Giant squid are mollusks, so they are related to octopuses, giant clams, and even garden snails!

TITANS
Whalers have caught sperm whales that had strange disklike wounds. Experts believe these were made by a giant squid's huge suckers as the whale tried to make a meal of the squid.

DATABANK

INPUT

Q What animals are known as crustaceans and which one is the largest in the world?

Q Is a starfish a species of fish or is it an invertebrate?

Q What is the most dangerous invertebrate to humans?

OUTPUT

A Crustaceans include crabs, lobsters, and shrimp. The largest is the spider crab.

A It is an invertebrate. Starfish are closely related to sea urchins and sea cucumbers.

A The mosquito. It spreads malaria, which kills thousands of people every year.

FINS AND SCALES

Fish, amphibians, and reptiles were the first vertebrates—animals with backbones. While fish live in water, reptiles survive on land. Amphibians live in the water and on land.

 ## Fish

Fish differ from other vertebrates because they have gills, allowing them to breathe underwater. There are 24,000 species of fish, 60 percent live in the sea. They range in size from a species of goby barely the length of a thumbnail to the 39 foot-long whale shark. Despite its name, the whale shark eats tiny fish and plankton and is not dangerous. Not all fish are confined to water. Flying fish leap out of the ocean escaping danger by gliding 1,300 feet along the water on stiff fins that act as wings. The African lungfish can survive four years encased in mud if the pond it lives in dries up; it breathes air using a primitive type of lung. When the rainy season comes, it crawls out of its sanctuary and looks for food.

Archerfish fire water at insects on overhanging leaves to shoot them down. The insects are then eaten.

FISH FATHERHOOD
A female seahorse lays eggs in a pouch on the male's body. He protects the young until they can fend for themselves.

DATABANK

Q How does an electric eel produce electricity and what does it use it for?

A The eel produces and stores electricity with special muscle cells called electroplaques. It uses this power to stun prey.

Q Which is the longest snake in the world?

A The reticulated python reaches up to 33 ft. in length.

POND PARENTS
A male stickleback (red) makes a nest and entices a female to lay her eggs inside it. He then guards the eggs and young.

FISH VOYAGE
The European eel migrates from the Sargasso Sea to Europe where it lives until adulthood. It returns to the Sargasso to breed. Eels go on land if their path is blocked.

North America
Europe
Africa
South America
Sargasso Sea
Atlantic Ocean

GREAT WHITE TRAGEDY
Feared because of films like *Jaws*, the great white shark is heavily hunted. Today, there are less than 5,000 left.

Reptiles

In the past, there were many different types of reptiles, but today there are only snakes, lizards, turtles, and crocodiles. A typical reptile has dry, scaly skin and lays eggs. Many lizards have a unique defense mechanism—if caught, they can break off their tail and escape. Later, it grows another tail. One species that has no such worries is the Komodo dragon. Reaching 10 feet long, it can hunt animals as large as water buffalo—and even humans.

CARING CROC
The saltwater crocodile is the largest living reptile. Despite appearances, it shows tenderness toward its young.

· Nearly one million people are bitten by snakes every year—40,000 result in death.

FULL THROTTLE
Boa constrictors kill prey, such as this nutria, by suffocation. As the animal tries to breathe, the snake squeezes tighter.

FACTS AND FIGURES

One giant tortoise lived from 1766 to 1918. It had survived for at least 152 years!

The sailfish swims at speeds over 62 mph—the fastest fish in the ocean.

The world's largest frog is the goliath frog. At 8 lbs., it is nearly the size of a chicken!

There are over 4,200 species of amphibians and about 6,800 species of reptiles.

Amphibians

While reptiles have tough skin, amphibians, like frogs, toads, and salamanders, have thin, moist skin and have to stay near water to avoid drying out. Most lay their eggs in water. At first, a young frog or toad is called a tadpole. It looks like a small fish and cannot survive on land. Over time, however, the tadpole's long tail shrinks and it develops legs and lungs. By the time it looks like its parents, it can breathe air and it spends increasingly long periods out of water. The world's largest amphibian is the giant salamander which reaches 6 feet long and 144 pounds.

A frog tadpole can grow to be 6 in. long, but as an adult it can be only 2–3 in. long!

DEADLY FROG
Poison dart frogs carry deadly toxins. A golden poison dart frog has enough poison to kill 1,000 people.

BIRDS

Birds are not only masters of the air but they have also conquered nearly every other habitat. They can be found roosting in mountain ranges, diving for fish in the ice cold seas of the Antarctic, or nesting in the bleakest deserts.

 ## Flying

Birds have three features that set them apart from other animals: feathers, hollow bones, and bills. Feathers make wings sturdy for flight and protect against heat and cold. Their bones are hollow, so they are light enough for flight; and the bills of different species are adapted to feed on all kinds of food, like seeds or meat. Birds have various methods of flight. The hummingbird hovers on wings that beat up to 90 times per second. The albatross glides without flapping its wings. The arctic tern also uses this energy-saving method to make the 10,000 mile annual trip from its breeding territory in the Arctic, to winter feeding grounds in the Antarctic—and back again. In a lifetime, this is equal to flying to the moon and back!

A pet budgie in California had a vocabulary of 1,728 human words.

SWEET FEAST
Hummingbirds have very long tongues and bills in order to reach the sugary nectar deep inside tropical flowers.

BIG BILL
The toucan's bill is up to half its length. The bill has internal struts to make it both strong and lightweight. The bright coloring is vital for attracting mates in the breeding season.

FACTS AND FIGURES

The prehistoric *Teratornis* was the biggest flying bird ever. It had a 20 ft. wingspan.

The smallest bird is the bee hummingbird. It is 2 in. long, including bill and tail.

The fastest flier is the peregrine falcon, which can dive at over 155 mph.

Birds such as geese and swans can fly at over 30,000 ft.—higher than Mt. Everest.

North American passenger pigeons, now extinct, lived in flocks of over 2 billion.

The red-billed quelea is the most populous bird today, with over 1.5 billion adults.

There are between 8,500 and 10,000 bird species in the world.

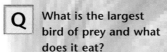

DATABANK

	INPUT		OUTPUT
Q	Why do birds such as swallows migrate each year?	A	Birds migrate long distances looking for fresh sources of food.
Q	What is the largest bird of prey and what does it eat?	A	The Andean condor, feeds on dead animals and reaches 27 lbs.
Q	What is the rarest bird and how many are left in the wild?	A	In 1999, only one Spix's macaw was living in the wild.
Q	What is the world's most dangerous bird to humans?	A	The cassowary, of Australia. It is 7 ft. tall and can kill a human.

Grounded

Some birds have lost the ability to fly. The ostrich, the world's largest bird, uses its muscular legs to run up to 40 mph in order to escape danger. Yet giving up flying can be risky. The dodo, from the island of Mauritius, had no enemies until sailors arrived and hunted it for food. It became extinct in 1662. The rare kakapo of New Zealand is a flightless parrot. It is endangered because its nests, which it builds on the ground, are raided by rats.

EGGSTREME
The ostrich lays eggs that weigh 4 lbs.— big enough to make 12 regular omelets.

Some birds rarely come to ground. Sooty terns remain airborne for up to 10 years and only land to breed.

Chick and Egg

Birds produce the widest variety of nests and eggs. The mute swan lays one of the biggest eggs, 5 inches long, of any flying bird. It needs a nest 5 feet wide to hold its eggs. In contrast, the vervain hummingbird lays a 1 centimeter long egg—a fraction of the size. While many newly-hatched chicks are helpless and take weeks to develop, the young malleefowl of southern Australia flies when it is only 24 hours old.

HELPLESS YOUNGSTER
It takes a chick hours to break out of its shell. Most baby birds depend on their parents for food for weeks after.

FOSTER CHICK
Cuckoos lay eggs in the nests of smaller birds. When it hatches, the chick is fed by the parents as if it was their own.

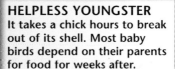

Birds of Prey

Birds of prey, like eagles, are efficient hunters. They have powerful claws in order to kill and carry off prey, and sharp bills with which to eat it. Eagles soar high above the land, using their sharp eyesight to locate food. The peregrine falcon, which catches other birds in midair, can spot its prey up to a remarkable 5 miles away.

A nest belonging to a pair of bald eagles in Florida weighed almost three tons.

CLEAN UP
Vultures feed on the carcasses of dead animals. By cleaning up, they prevent diseases from spreading.

MAMMALS

There are over 4,000 species of mammals, in all shapes and sizes. They are found all over the world, and have mastered the sea and air, as well as the land.

 ## Mammal World

The world's smallest mammal is Kitti's hognosed bat from Thailand, which weighs .07 ounces—less than a ping-pong ball. It would take 75 million of these bumblebee-sized bats to equal the weight of the world's largest mammal, the blue whale. On land, African elephants are the heavyweight champions, but the largest hunters are polar bears. With their thick coats of fur, they endure temperatures as low as −40°F, traveling up to 740 miles a year across the ice in search of food. The addax, a small antelope, braves the heat of the Sahara Desert where the midday temperature can reach 122°F. It survives by getting all the water it needs from the plants it eats. Both the addax and the polar bear live in small groups, but some mammals gather in huge herds. In eastern Africa, about 2 million wildebeest and 300,000 plains zebras migrate thousands of miles between feeding grounds every year. Today many mammal species are endangered. There are only about 700 giant pandas left in China because of the destruction of bamboo—their primary food—in their forest home.

A female true lemming can become pregnant at the age of just 14 days and give birth 16 days later.

LAND GIANT
The biggest African elephant weighs about 12 tons—much more than a bus full of passengers.

There are an estimated 5.3 billion rats in the world—almost 1 rat for every human being.

HUNTED HUNTER
At 9 ft. long, the tiger is the largest cat. It has been heavily hunted and less than 5,000 now survive in the wild.

FACTS AND FIGURES

The rarest large mammal is the Javan rhinoceros. There are less than 70 in the wild.

At 20 ft. tall, the giraffe can peer through the window of a third-floor apartment.

The koala is one of the sleepiest mammals. It spends 22 hours a day dozing.

The fastest mammal is the cheetah. This hunting cat reaches 62 mph.

The fin whale may live to be 90 years old, making it the longest-lived wild mammal.

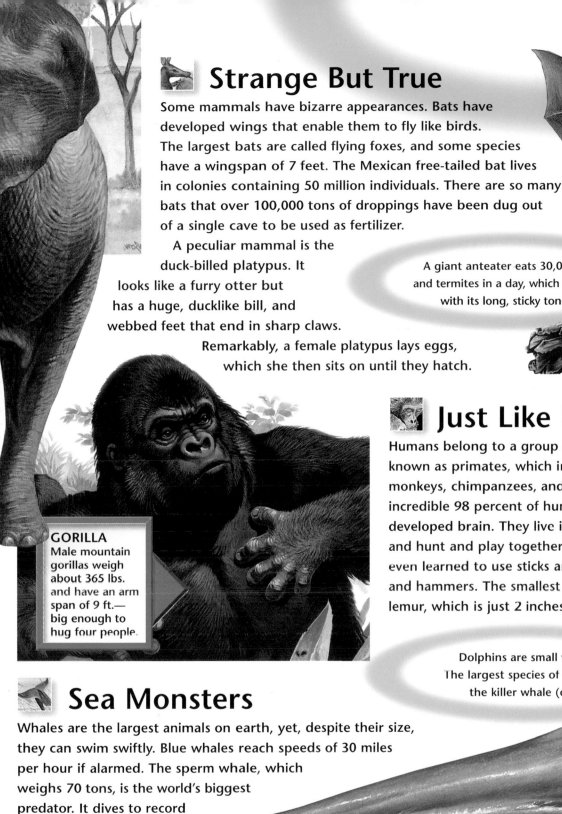

Strange But True

Some mammals have bizarre appearances. Bats have developed wings that enable them to fly like birds. The largest bats are called flying foxes, and some species have a wingspan of 7 feet. The Mexican free-tailed bat lives in colonies containing 50 million individuals. There are so many bats that over 100,000 tons of droppings have been dug out of a single cave to be used as fertilizer.

A peculiar mammal is the duck-billed platypus. It looks like a furry otter but has a huge, ducklike bill, and webbed feet that end in sharp claws. Remarkably, a female platypus lays eggs, which she then sits on until they hatch.

A giant anteater eats 30,000 ants and termites in a day, which it catches with its long, sticky tongue.

FRUIT BATTY
Almost a quarter of all mammal species are bats. Some eat insects, while others feed on fruit.

Just Like Us

Humans belong to a group of mammals known as primates, which include monkeys, chimpanzees, and gorillas. Chimps share an incredible 98 percent of human genes and have a well-developed brain. They live in complex family groups, and hunt and play together. Some individuals have even learned to use sticks and rocks as tools, like chisels and hammers. The smallest primate is the mouse lemur, which is just 2 inches long, with a 5 inch tail.

GORILLA
Male mountain gorillas weigh about 365 lbs. and have an arm span of 9 ft.— big enough to hug four people.

Dolphins are small whales. The largest species of dolphin is the killer whale (orca).

Sea Monsters

Whales are the largest animals on earth, yet, despite their size, they can swim swiftly. Blue whales reach speeds of 30 miles per hour if alarmed. The sperm whale, which weighs 70 tons, is the world's biggest predator. It dives to record depths of 10,000 feet hunting fish. Walruses and seals are also at home at sea. The crab-eater seal is the most populous large sea mammal; there are 30 million in Antarctica.

BIGGEST IN THE WORLD
The longest blue whale ever caught was measured at 110 ft. from head to tail. The heaviest whale weighed 190 tons.

INTO THE PAST

In ancient and medieval times, great civilizations rose and fell. Some lasted for hundreds of years and left a deep impression on history by shaping today's laws, customs, and politics.

Egyptians

Egypt was one of the world's first great civilizations. It rose 5,000 years ago and lasted for 3,000 years until it was absorbed into the Roman Empire. The Nile River regularly flooded, producing fertile land that gave the Egyptians the wealth to build great monuments and to establish a highly sophisticated society. Egyptians developed the calendar and also invented hieroglyphics—a form of writing based on pictures.

CEREMONY
Ancient Egypt's supreme god was Amun. His throned statue was lavished with gifts during religious rites.

In Egypt, the king was treated as a god and had total power over his many subjects.

MUMMY
An Egyptian king's body was soaked in spices and wrapped in linen bandages to preserve it for the afterlife.

Classical Times

Ancient Greece was made up of independent city states, such as Thebes, Sparta, and Athens, which came to prominence 500–150 B.C. Greek culture inspired enlightened thinkers like Aristotle and Plato, and writers including Euripides and Sophocles. The works of these individuals still influence modern politics, literature, art, and science. Like Egypt, Greece was eventually conquered by the Romans. The Romans were noted soldiers and administrators, but their culture was based on Greek ideas, which they allowed to spread throughout their massive empire.

ROME'S RISE
At its height, the Roman Empire extended from Britain to Egypt and from Spain to the Caspian Sea in Asia.

Europe
• Londinium (London)
• Lutetia (Paris)
Asia
Caspian Sea
• Rome
• Athens
• Carthage
Africa
• Jerusalem
• Alexandria

ENLIGHTENED
Greek culture was able to flourish without outside threat after the Greek states, led by Athens, defeated the invading Persians at Marathon in 490 B.C. and Salamis in 480 B.C.

FACTS AND FIGURES

The Chinese first used explosives in battle in 1161 at the battle of Ts'ai-shih.

Rome, with a population of 1 million in A.D. 100, was the largest city of its age.

The oldest evidence of the domestication of animals dates from 8650 B.C. and was found in Iraq.

King Henry V of England beat a French army of 25,000 at Agincourt in 1415 with only 6,000 men.

DATABANK

Q Which is the oldest town in the world, and how many people lived there?

A Jericho dates from at least 9000 B.C. By 8000 B.C., it held 2,000 people. The site is still inhabited.

Q Is it true that part of the Roman Empire survived the fall of Rome itself?

A The Eastern Empire lasted until 1453. Constantinople (now Istanbul, Turkey) was its capital.

Middle Ages

The fall of the Roman Empire in about A.D. 500 was followed by the conquest of the Mediterranean 200 years later by Arab Muslims. While Europe entered a period of disorder, Arab areas of influence, particularly Spain, saw a great revival of learning. The Arab army, of 80,000, was finally halted at the Battle of Tours, in France, in A.D. 732 by the 40,000 strong forces of the Christian king Charles Martel. The Christian kings of Europe, led by the Pope, followed with the "reconquest" of Spain, and launched crusades to "free" the Holy Land. In the Far East, war and invasion were also common. The Chinese empire, another area of great learning, was conquered by Genghis Khan's nomadic Mongols in 1234. These warriors overran Asia and even threatened Europe, reaching Vienna in 1241, before turning back after the death of their leader.

HIGH SOCIETY Mayans had a sophisticated civilization in the mountains of Central and South America, A.D. 250–1650.

LANCE A LOT Tournaments were the athletic competitions of the Middle Ages, helping knights practice key battle skills.

Of the nine crusades to the Holy Land only the first (1096–99) succeeded in its aim of capturing Jerusalem.

JOUSTING Charging knights used lances to unseat their opponents. A knight was declared to be the loser once he fell off his horse.

HISTORICAL FIGURES

History is filled with colorful characters. Some were great warriors or fierce tyrants who stamped their mark on history, others are remembered for their inspirational deeds and words.

 ## Ancient Thinkers

Greeks like Aristotle, Archimedes, and Plato, and the Islamic philosopher Averroës shaped much of western scientific and philosophical thought. Aristotle is one of history's great jack-of-all-trades—he was an expert in logic, ethics, politics, psychology, physics, biology, *and* poetry! In the East, Chinese philosopher Confucius (551–479 B.C.) developed ideas that became the official state philosophy of China.

CONFUCIUS
The name Confucius is Latin for K'ung-Fu-tzu. He was a Chinese minister who became a wandering sage.

Archimedes was killed when, immersed in a math problem, he ignored an attacking Roman soldier.

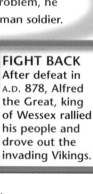

 ## Defenders

The most popular leaders have been those who defend their people, usually against great odds or injustice. In Egypt, around 3,500 years ago, the Hebrew people were subject to the tyrannic rule of the pharaohs—until Moses came to lead them. According to legend, Moses parted the Red Sea to enable his people to escape. He led the Hebrews through many hardships before they reached the promised land of Israel. Boudicca, Queen of the Iceni tribe in ancient Britain, valiantly led her people against Roman occupation in A.D. 61. After several victories, including the burning of London, her forces were crushed. Boudicca drank poison to avoid being captured.

FIGHT BACK
After defeat in A.D. 878, Alfred the Great, king of Wessex rallied his people and drove out the invading Vikings.

As well as being a great resistance fighter, Alfred the great encouraged learning and promoted justice.

MARTYR
In 1429, Joan of Arc led the French to victory against the English who were besieging Orléans. Later she was betrayed and burned at the stake for "sorcery."

CIVIL WARRIOR
One of Abraham Lincoln's reasons for fighting the South in the Civil War (1861–65) was to abolish slavery.

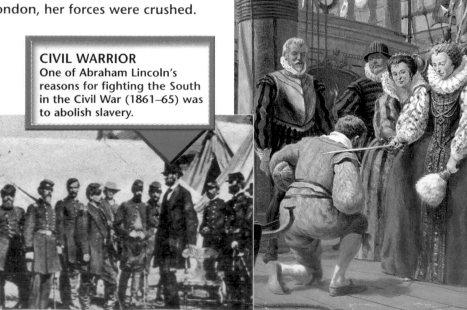

MIGHTY EMPIRE
Genghis Khan's army was mostly cavalry. On horseback, they could launch swift attacks, killing armies of foot soldiers.

Conquerors

In the past, conquest and victory in battle was a way of gaining wealth and uniting a nation. A successful conqueror was popular. One of the most feared was the Mongol Genghis Khan (1162–1227). He rose from obscurity to unify the semi-barbaric tribes of Mongolia, massacring his enemies. When he defeated the Tartars, he killed everyone "above the height of a cart axle." The Mongols went on to conquer China at a cost of millions of lives. Another formidable general, Napoleon Bonaparte (1769–1821) led France's armies to victory at Austerlitz (1805) and Jena (1806). For a few years, he held all of Europe except Britain. He was eventually captured at the Battle of Waterloo (1815) and exiled to the island of St. Helena in the Atlantic Ocean.

Ivan IV of Russia (1530–84) was known as Ivan the Terrible because he was a strong, crafty, and cruel ruler.

LEGENDARY
One of the greatest generals the world has ever seen, Alexander the Great conquered an empire from Greece to India by 326 B.C.—a feat a modern army would find hard to match.

FACTS AND FIGURES

Julius Caesar led the Romans to conquer Gaul (France) in 58 B.C. making Rome the controlling force in the West.

English king Henry VIII had six different wives during his 38-year reign.

Mary Queen of Scots became queen of Scotland when she was just one week old.

Attila, king of the Huns, massacred, looted, and took slaves in eastern Europe (433–441).

George Washington became the first President of the U.S. in 1789.

FAIR QUEEN
Elizabeth I's English fleet defeated the Spanish Armada in 1585, keeping England independent.

SNOW WAY FORWARD
Napoleon invaded Russia in 1812, but was forced back by terrible weather. Much of his powerful army froze to death.

EXPLORERS

Throughout history, adventurers have risked their lives crossing strange countries and seas in search of new lands, fame, and fortune. For many, however, death was their only reward.

GOOD COOK
James Cook insured that his ship's crew ate a balanced diet so they did not succumb to diseases like scurvy. Cook was killed by natives on the island of Hawaii in 1779.

 ## Australia

The first explorers to reach Australia may have been the Chinese in the 1400s. In the 1500s, Portuguese and Spanish explorers claimed to have discovered *terra australis incognita*—the "unknown southern land." By 1642, Dutch navigators, in particular Abel Tasman, had mapped Australia's western coast, Tasmania, and New Zealand. However, it was Captain James Cook who charted Australia's eastern coast, claiming the new lands for England in 1770. Cook made several more voyages in the Pacific and even ventured as far south as Antarctica.

The first settlers of Australia were the Aboriginal people who arrived from Asia some 40,000 years ago.

In 1912, Captain Robert Scott perished during his expedition to reach the South Pole.

FACTS AND FIGURES

In 1953, Edmund Hillary and Norgay Tenzing became the first to climb Mt. Everest.

The first journey to the South Pole was made in 1911 by Roald Amundsen of Norway.

Vasco da Gama of Portugal sailed around the Cape of Good Hope to India in 1497.

Juan Sebastián del Cano of Spain was the first to sail around the world, 1519–22.

In 1909, American Robert Peary became the first man to reach the North Pole.

Amerigo Vespucci, from Italy, explored the coast of South America 1499–1501.

 ## Marco Polo

In the early Middle Ages, Europeans knew little about China and the Far East except through travelers' tales brought back by traders. In 1271, however, the Venetian merchant, Marco Polo, set off with his father and uncle on an epic expedition that was to open people's eyes. After crossing Turkey, Iran, Afghanistan, India, and most of China, the Polos spent 17 years as guests of the Mongol Emperor Kublai Khan, visiting places never before seen by Europeans. Marco wrote down his experiences when he returned home. Although many people did not believe him, merchants were encouraged to travel east and seek their fortunes.

SEASONED TRAVELERS
Even after they had reached China, the Polos spent many years exploring the vast provinces of the Mongol Empire.

GO EAST
It took the Polos four years to reach China. They had to cross several mountain ranges and endure dry, inhospitable deserts filled with wild animals and armed bandits.

The New World

Exactly which European first discovered the Americas is the subject of great debate. Viking sagas tell of Leif Ericsson who landed on the North American continent in A.D. 1000. He named it "Vinland" because of the wild grapes he found growing there. Remains of a Viking settlement have been discovered in Newfoundland, Canada. However, the man most commonly credited with discovering both North and South America is Christopher Columbus. Born in Genoa, Italy, Columbus believed that he could find a shortcut to Asia, or the Indies, by sailing west across the Atlantic Ocean.

Columbus believed he had landed in the East Indies, so he called the Native Americans "Indians."

HUMAN WORLD

UNSETTLED
Vikings tried to set up a colony in "Vinland." They had to abandon their plans three years later because of hostility from Native North Americans.

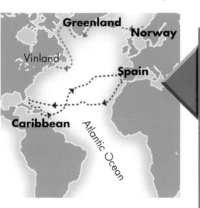

LAND AHOY!
Columbus (red) sailed across the Atlantic to the Carribean. The Vikings (blue) stayed closer to the coasts. They found North America when a storm blew one of their ships far off course.

Columbus had difficulty gaining support for his expedition, but he finally set sail in August 1492. In October, after a perilous voyage, he reached what was probably the Bahamas. He then visited Cuba and Haiti before heading home. On later voyages, Columbus reached the Gulf of Mexico and South America. However, it was John Cabot, also from Italy, who discovered the North American mainland in 1497.

SMALL SQUADRON
Columbus's ships were called the *Santa Maria*, the *Niña*, and the *Pinta*. Their combined crews totalled only 120 men.

REVOLUTION AND WAR

Revolutions change the social, political, and economic structure of a country. But the most extensive changes are brought about by war, which can devastate entire regions and populations.

BRITS OUT
The American colonies revolted against British rule in 1775 because of high, oppressive taxes.

 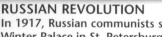

Revolutions

Revolutions occur when a country's people are suffering hardship. If people believe their leaders contribute to their suffering, their anger may become a violent uprising. Retaliation can be severe. The peasant revolts in England in 1381 and in Germany in 1525 were brutally put down by the landowners.

After a major war with Britain, the Treaty of Paris gave the American colonies their independence in 1783.

RUSSIAN REVOLUTION
In 1917, Russian communists seized the Winter Palace in St. Petersburg, removing the old, corrupt monarchy.

FACTS AND FIGURES

Simón Bolívar (1783–1830) led revolts in Venezuela, Columbia, Ecuador, and Peru.

In China, those opposed to the government during the Cultural Revolution were killed or tortured.

Many modern ideas of freedom and democracy stem from the French Revolution.

Up to 65 million soldiers were mobilized in World War I. 8.5 million were killed.

The Vietnam War (1955–75) claimed the lives of over 2 million Vietnamese people.

The Iran-Iraq War of 1980–88 led to 500,000 casualties with little gain.

Tanks were used for the first time in 1916. They made it easier to attack in battle.

Off With Her Head

In 1789, France was ruled by a corrupt government and king, Louis XVI, who spent a lot of money on luxuries. Meanwhile, people starved—harvests failed and food prices rose. They demanded justice. Riots broke out in many areas, members of the ruling class were murdered, and the king was arrested in 1792 to be executed a year later. The old political system was replaced by the Republic, which aimed for "liberty, equality, and fraternity" for all. But it was followed by the Reign of Terror—a ten-month period of execution and murder—until a moderate government took control.

THE TERROR
Up to 20,000 "enemies of the Revolution" were beheaded on the guillotine during the Reign of Terror.

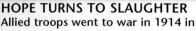

Conflict

War is a conflict between the armies of nations, states, or between groups within a country (known as a civil war). Wars start for many reasons. A country may attack another to gain land, wealth, or revenge. Wars are violent and many die. The United Nations was set up in 1945 to try to prevent wars.

MASS DESTRUCTION
War in the 1900s led to the creation of deadly weapons, like Germany's *V2* rocket used in World War II.

CIVIL WAR
The Civil War (1861–65) was fought between groups of states, mainly the North and the South.

TRENCHES
In World War I, soldiers dug trenches for protection from enemy fire. Trenches were hard to attack.

HOPE TURNS TO SLAUGHTER
Allied troops went to war in 1914 in high spirits. By September 1918, millions of them had died in grim trench warfare.

World War I

World War I (1914–18) was caused by distrust between the major powers at the time. The Allies—France, U.S.S.R., and the British Empire, with help later from Italy and the U.S., fought against Germany, Austria-Hungary, and Turkey. The Allies prevailed, but many lives were lost. The terms of the peace treaty of 1919 then led to World War II.

World War II

In 1939, the German army invaded Poland as part of the Nazis' plan to create a German empire. This forced the U.K. and France to declare war on Germany. The Nazis, allied with Italy and later Japan, went on to conquer most of Europe. In 1941, the U.S. entered the war and in 1942 the Soviet Union defeated the Germans at Stalingrad. However, peace was not achieved until 1945.

World War II led to the Cold War— a long period of tension between Russia and the U.S.

FLATTENED IN AN INSTANT
Japan fought until August 1945 when the U.S. dropped atom bombs on Hiroshima and Nagasaki, killing 200,000 people.

20TH-CENTURY LEADERS

Some of the most famous and important people of the last century were our leaders. They took us into world wars, brought us peace, and continue to hold enormous influence over our lives.

Politicians

MISSILE CRISIS
This cartoon shows Soviet leader Krushchev and President Kennedy, close to nuclear war, in 1962.

The British prime minister Winston Churchill led the fight against Germany, Italy, and Japan during World War II (1939–45). A formidable tactician, Churchill was also a great public speaker—his stirring speeches encouraged people in Nazi-occupied Europe to resist Hitler. John F. Kennedy is probably the world's most famous peacetime leader. Elected in 1960—one of the youngest U.S. presidents—he is best remembered for supporting civil rights. After bringing the world to the brink of nuclear war in 1962 during the Cuban missile crisis, he improved relations between the U.S.S.R. and the U.S., achieving a nuclear test ban.

WORLD WAR II ALLIES
Churchill, President Roosevelt, and Stalin, leader of Russia, met at Yalta in the Crimea, in 1945.

FACTS AND FIGURES

The first ever female prime minister was Sri Lanka's Sirimavo Bandaranaike, 1960.

It is claimed that there may have been 600 attempts to kill Cuban leader Fidel Castro.

Pedro Lascurain was president of Mexico for one hour in 1913 before resigning.

Margaret Thatcher became the first woman prime minister of Britain in 1979.

Tibet's leader, the Dalai Lama, has been in exile since China invaded Tibet in 1950.

Franklin D. Roosevelt was president for 12 years—the longest serving U.S. president.

Freedom Fighters

The last century saw many crusaders for human rights. In India, Gandhi used nonviolent protest to win independence for India from the British Empire in 1948. Nelson Mandela, head of the African National Congress, fought against South Africa's racist apartheid policy. Imprisoned by the government in 1964, he was finally released in 1990, and a year later apartheid was abolished. With South African president F. W. de Clerk, Mandela won the Nobel Peace Prize in 1993, and in 1994 he became South Africa's first black president.

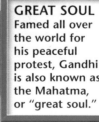

GREAT SOUL
Famed all over the world for his peaceful protest, Gandhi is also known as the Mahatma, or "great soul."

"I HAVE A DREAM"
Influenced by Gandhi, Dr. Martin Luther King, Jr. became a figurehead for civil rights in the U.S. during the 1960s.

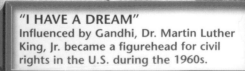

FASCIST ALLY
Benito Mussolini became dictator of Italy in 1922. He was an ally of Hitler in World War II and was killed in 1945.

Hitler and other top Nazis committed suicide to avoid capture by their enemies.

Dictators

Dictators are leaders with unlimited power. Adolf Hitler of Germany was the most infamous modern dictator. His attempts to create a huge empire in Europe led to World War II. The conflict caused worldwide suffering and over 50 million people died. He was defeated in 1945 by the allies (the U.S., Britain, and the U.S.S.R.). Soviet leader, Joseph Stalin, was also a powerful dictator. Stalin came to power in 1922 and ordered many bloody purges to secure his leadership. Responsible for over ten million deaths during his long rule, Stalin was never overthrown, and died in power in 1953.

DATABANK

INPUT	OUTPUT
Q Does France have a king or queen?	**A** No. France has an elected president as the head of state.
Q Who was General Francisco Franco and where did he rule?	**A** An ally of Hitler, Franco was dictator of Spain, 1939–75.
Q Who was the last British royal to be assassinated?	**A** Lord Mountbatten was killed by Irish terrorists in 1979.
Q What was Ronald Reagan before he became U.S. president?	**A** Reagan was originally an actor. He starred in 50 films.

HOLOCAUST
Hitler murdered millions of innocent people, including over six million Jews in concentration camps in Europe.

Russia and its empire used to be known as the U.S.S.R.—the Union of Soviet Socialist Republics.

Assassination

Leaders have been murdered for political or religious reasons. Human rights leaders Gandhi and Martin Luther King were both killed by angry extremists. In India, Rajiv Gandhi—no relation to Mahatma Gandhi—succeeded his mother Indira as prime minister after her assassination in 1984. However, he, too, was murdered by political enemies in 1991.

ARCHDUKE FRANZ FERDINAND
Ferdinand, heir to the throne of Austria, was assassinated in 1914 by Gavrilo Princip, a Slav nationalist. His death sparked off World War I.

THE ROMANOVS
Czar Nicholas II of Russia was forced to give up his throne after the 1917 revolution. A short time later, he and his entire family were shot.

PRESIDENT JOHN F. KENNEDY
Perhaps the most famous U.S. president, John F. Kennedy was assassinated in Dallas in 1963 by Lee Harvey Oswald.

INSIDE THE BODY

The body is a well-oiled machine. It appears smooth on the surface, but beneath the skin muscles flex, the lungs inflate, the heart pumps, and blood rushes to all parts of the body in order to keep us alive.

PUSH AND PULL
Muscles make up about half of the body's weight. If a muscle becomes damaged, it can repair itself.

SOFT CENTER
Bones have a spongy core. This contains red bone marrow, a soft tissue that produces blood cells.

A human body is made up of 50 trillion cells. There are 100,000 genes in each cell.

FACTS AND FIGURES

The heart beats over two billion times in a lifetime without stopping.

The digestive system, from the mouth to the anus, is about 30 ft. long.

The brain usually weighs about 3 lbs., but the heaviest recorded brain was 5 lbs.

A baby's heartbeat reaches 130 beats a minute—twice the rate of an adult heart.

The brain needs roughly its own weight in blood every minute to function.

Every day we breathe in and out about 25,000 times— over 17 times a minute.

 ## Muscles

There are over 640 muscles in the body and they provide the force that enables us to move. Just walking requires the use of 200 of them. Constructed of strong, flexible fibers, muscles are attached to bones by cords called tendons. The largest tendon in the body is the Achilles tendon, which connects the calf muscle to the heel bone. A muscle works by contracting—getting shorter—and pulling the bone it is attached to. After contracting, the muscle cannot straighten itself and has to be pulled back by another muscle. Therefore, muscles often work in pairs to move a bone back and forth.

Much of a baby's skeleton is flexible cartilage. As the child grows, bone replaces the cartilage.

 ## Skeleton

Like iron girders in a building, bones are the frames for our bodies. Without them we would collapse in a heap. Although they look dead, bones are living structures with blood vessels and nerves. There are 206 bones in the body and they come in all shapes and sizes. The longest and toughest is the thighbone, which is about five times the strength of steel. The smallest is the stirrup bone in the ear, which aids hearing. It is only 0.2 inches long.

SKULL
There are 22 bones in the skull. Eight bones protect the brain, and 14 make up the face.

HANDY WORK
Our hands and forearms contain over 30 muscles. These enable us to perform many intricate tasks with our fingers.

THE HEART OF THE MATTER
About the size of a grapefruit, the heart beats 60–80 times a minute. This rises to over 100 during vigorous exercise.

Circulation

Blood acts like a transportation system. Each drop holds 250 million red blood cells that ferry food and oxygen around the body and remove waste. Each day, 170 billion blood cells are produced; 2 million blood cells die every second. The heart pumps blood through arteries so that blood reaches every organ in the body. If all the body's blood vessels were laid out end-to-end, they would be 100,000 miles long.

When blood reaches the lungs, it takes in the fresh oxygen that we have just breathed in, and releases a waste gas, carbon dioxide, which we then breathe out. The blood carries the oxygen and food from the stomach to every cell in the body.

LIFE LINE
Arteries (red) circulate blood rich in oxygen. Veins (blue) take oxygen-poor blood to the heart and lungs.

When the body is resting, it takes about a minute for the blood to make one circuit of the body.

DATABANK

INPUT	OUTPUT
Q How many quarts of blood are there flowing in the body?	**A** Adults have about 5 qts. of blood. This would fill half a pail.
Q How many kidneys are there and what are they used for?	**A** The two kidneys rid the blood of waste and excrete urine.
Q What's the difference between white and red blood cells?	**A** Red cells carry oxygen and food; white cells defend against germs.
Q What happens to the body when the heart stops beating?	**A** Without blood, body tissues die. The brain is affected first.

Brain

The brain is the body's control center. It enables us to move, to think, and to learn, and is far more powerful than the most complex computer. Although the brain accounts for only 2 percent of the body's weight, it needs 20 percent of the body's blood. It sends messages to the body along nerves, which act like telephone wires. Moving at 200 miles per hour, these impulses tell muscles to move, instruct the heart to pump, and make sure that we keep breathing. Impulses also carry information from every part of the body back to the brain.

THE SENSES

The senses give us all our information about the outside world. They enable us to see and touch our surroundings, to hear sounds around us, and to smell and taste what we eat.

 ## Sight

Sight is the most complex sense. When we look at something, light from that object enters our eyes. The cornea and lens focus the light onto the 130 million light-sensitive cells in the retina at the back of the eye. These cells are split into two groups: the rods detect general shape and movement and the cones detect detail and color. The image that forms is upside down, but the information is sent via the optic nerve to the brain, which correctly interprets the image.

WINDOW ON THE WORLD
The iris acts like the aperture of a camera, enlarging and reducing the pupil—the hole that allows light to enter the eye.

Lens

Iris

Cornea

Pupil

Optic nerve   Retina

 ## Touch

The touch-sensitive nerve endings embedded in our skin are the most widespread of the sense organs, covering the whole body. There are five main types of touch receptors, each of which detects a different form of sensation. Touch is measured with an esthesiometer, an instrument that looks like a drawing compass with two needle points.

INSECTS
Insects, like the dragonfly, have compound eyes with up to 30,000 facets. These facets do not produce many views but create a single, panoramic, if a little grainy, image.

BRAILLE DOTS
Braille is composed of groups of raised dots that allow blind people to read by using touch.

FACTS AND FIGURES

The semicircular canals in the inner ear detect movement of the body and help us balance.

Elephants communicate using subsonic sounds—far below the range of human hearing.

Men are 20 times more likely to be color-blind (unable to tell colors apart) than women.

The small nasal cavity contains around 12 million smell receptors.

Dogs hear sounds at 35,000 hertz—double the highest frequency audible to humans.

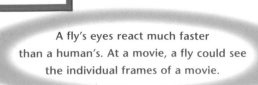

A fly's eyes react much faster than a human's. At a movie, a fly could see the individual frames of a movie.

Taste and Smell

Our senses of taste and smell are closely linked. These senses work by detecting chemicals in food and in the air, so they are also known as chemosenses. In some animals, the two senses are combined—snakes use their tongues to taste for scents in the air. Our sense of taste is limited to four basic chemical reactions. This is compensated for by our ability to detect over 10,000 different "smell" chemicals, which enhance our impression of the taste of food in our mouth. Children have a more acute sense of smell than adults, but this sense slowly weakens with age as the smell receptors die off.

Some people have synaesthesia—their senses are confused. A sound may be interpreted as a color!

Bitter   Sweet

Sour   Salty

TASTE BUDS
The tongue has over 10,000 taste buds, but only identifies four tastes—salty, sour, sweet, and bitter. Each is detected by taste buds located in a specific area of the tongue.

Sound travels in waves. The number of sound waves each second is called its frequency and is measured in hertz.

Fish have a different sense. A line of nerves along the side of their body detects vibrations in the water.

SOUND SENSE
Bats use a form of sonar. By listening for the echoes of their squeaks they can locate their prey in the dark.

DATABANK

Q	How do we move our eyes in their sockets?
A	Each eyeball is attached to six sets of muscles that control the direction of its gaze.
Q	Which areas of the body are most sensitive to touch?
A	The face, mouth, hands, and feet have the largest number of touch receptors in the body.

Hearing

Our sense of hearing can detect a very wide range of sound frequencies—from deep rumbling noises at 30 hertz to high-pitched squeals at 18,000 hertz. Sound enters the outer ear and vibrates the eardrum. Sensitive hairs—about 240,000 of them—within the cochlea convert these vibrations into electrical signals. The signals are sent along nerve paths to the brain, where they are interpreted as sounds.

Nerve

Cochlea

Semicircular canal

TUBEWAY
The ear is linked to the throat by the Eustachian tube, which relieves buildups of pressure in the ear.

Ear canal

Eardrum

Pinna (gathers sounds)

MEDICINE

Today, people are living longer than ever. Treatments have been found for some "incurable" diseases and surgical expertise saves millions of lives a year.

Disease

Before the 1900s, serious infectious diseases, such as smallpox and diphtheria were usually fatal. Caused by organisms that attack the body, such as bacteria, diseases spread easily from person to person. Today, medicines and improved hygiene have eradicated or contained many of the worst diseases. Now, the biggest killers are non-infectious diseases, like cancer. In the developed world, cancer kills 1,000 per 100,000 people, compared to 5 per 100,000 people for infectious diseases.

MOSQUITO MENACE
The malaria virus is carried by mosquitos, which spread the disease to humans. Malaria kills over a million people a year.

Diseases of the heart and blood account for over 50 percent of deaths in developed Western nations.

BLACK DEATH
Carried by rat fleas, bubonic plague (the Black Death) killed up to half of Europe's population in the mid-1300s.

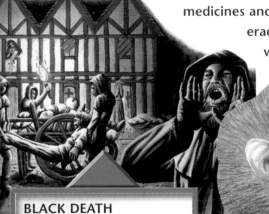

COUGHS AND SNEEZES
Up to 22 million people died in the influenza (flu) epidemic that struck worldwide after World War I.

Diagnosis

Doctors have existed for thousands of years. The *Code of Hammurabi* from Babylon (1800 B.C.) is a text about medical practices. Many people believed that illnesses were punishments and could only be cured using magic. Ancient Greek physicians, like Hippocrates, challenged this. He used observation and logic to understand illnesses and provide effective treatment, although his knowledge was limited because the Greeks did not permit experiments on dead bodies. It was hundreds of years later that scientists like William Harvey (1578–1657) learned how the body worked by dissecting animals and humans. Harvey realized through his research how blood circulates.

AHEAD OF HIS TIME
Hippocrates (460–377 B.C.) knew that fresh air, exercise, and cleanliness were vital for health—just like we do today!

Andreas Vesalius (1514–64) of Belgium studied human anatomy using the bodies of executed criminals.

ASPIRIN
The ancient Egyptians used tea made from willow bark, which contains aspirin, to relieve pain.

HIPPOCRATIS COI
Genuina effigies ex antiquo numismate graeco Constantinopoli reperto

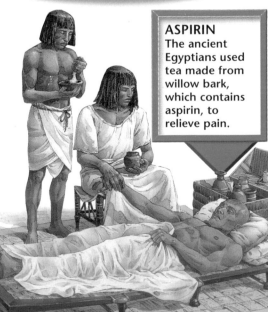

ROSY PERIWINKLE
Once thought worthless, now the rosy periwinkle from Madagascar's rain forests is used in medicines to treat leukemia.

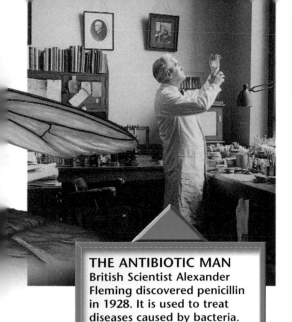

THE ANTIBIOTIC MAN
British Scientist Alexander Fleming discovered penicillin in 1928. It is used to treat diseases caused by bacteria.

BRAIN SCAN
Modern scanners can "see" deep inside the body and even look at the brain in detail, finding any problems.

Vaccines

British doctor Edward Jenner (1749–1823) discovered the first vaccine. He noticed that people who suffered from cowpox did not catch the deadly smallpox. To test this, he infected a boy with cowpox before exposing him to smallpox. The boy remained healthy—by fighting off the milder disease, his body built up defenses against smallpox. Using this knowledge, scientists created a smallpox vaccine that was eventually used worldwide. It was so successful that by 1979, the disease was eliminated.

Surgical Breakthroughs

Operations were so dangerous 150 years ago that most people died, usually of shock. Doctors gave their patients anesthetics, such as wine and laughing gas, to numb pain. But even when effective anesthetics were used, patients still died. Scottish surgeon Joseph Lister (1828–1912) realized that germs were the problem. After he ordered that everything, including the doctors, must be kept scrupulously clean, fewer people died. Another major breakthrough came with the first use of the heart-lung machine in 1953. A heart could be stopped while the machine took over, giving surgeons time to operate. In the 1960s, surgeons began transplanting hearts and other organs.

FACTS AND FIGURES

The AIDS virus was discovered in 1984 by a French scientist and two American scientists.

The first successful heart transplant was performed in South Africa in 1967.

Blood transfusions were attempted in Italy in the 1600s, but were later banned.

French chemist Louis Pasteur (1822–95) developed vaccines for anthrax and rabies.

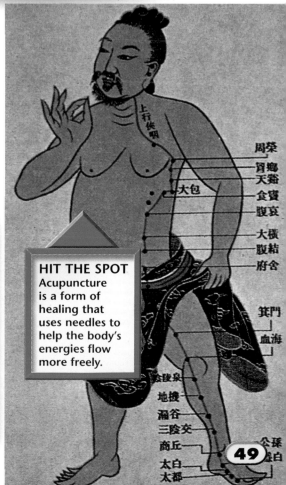

HIT THE SPOT
Acupuncture is a form of healing that uses needles to help the body's energies flow more freely.

DATABANK

INPUT

Q What is the most dangerous health threat today?

Q Are many diseases prevented with vaccines?

Q How many people are affected by cancer worldwide?

Q Who discovered X rays and when?

OUTPUT

A Tobacco-related illnesses are the most urgent health problem.

A Vaccines exist for polio, measles, influenza, and many more.

A 25 percent of the people in the developed world, less elsewhere.

A German Wilhelm Röentgen discovered X rays in 1895.

49

TRACK AND FIELD

Track and field consists of field events, which include long jump, high jump, shot put, discus and javelin throws, and track events, which involve running over various distances.

 ## The Olympics

Held every four years, the Olympic Games, with track and field events at its core, are the world's greatest sports events. The Olympics began at Olympia in ancient Greece, and records of it exist from as early as 776 B.C. It was a religious festival, but winning was very important. The modern Olympics began in Athens, Greece in 1896, instigated by Frenchman Pierre de Coubertin. He believed that competition and exercise in the form of sports and games were vital for all. It was not until 1928, however, that women were officially allowed to compete. In ancient times, winners received an olive wreath, but today they are awarded a gold medal.

RINGS OF PEACE
The Olympic rings represent the five inhabited continents and symbolize the international nature of the modern Games.

PASS IT ON
Relay team members take a baton, run part of the race with it, then pass the baton to their teammates.

In A.D. 393, Roman emperor Theodosius I prohibited pagan worship, including the Olympics!

 ## On Your Mark

Running events range from the 100-meters to the marathon, which is 26 miles long. Sprinters, like Maurice Greene and Marion Jones (winners of the men's and women's 100-meter run at the World Championships in 1999) use power and pure speed. Long-distance runners rely on stamina. African runners, such as Ethiopia's Haile Gebrselassie, regularly dominate events over 800 meters.

GREAT BRIT
A great British 100-meter runner, Linford Christie, won the Olympic title in 1992 and the world title in 1993. He lost his Olympic title in 1996 to Canada's Donovan Bailey.

QUICK MILE
In 1954, Britain's Roger Bannister became the first man to run a mile in less than four minutes. Today, athletes train harder than ever and the world record is 17 seconds quicker!

HASSIBA BOULMERKA
This Algerian won the 1,500-meter run in 1991 in Tokyo—becoming the first African woman to win a world title.

Field Events

Field events—jumping and throwing disciplines—take place in the space within the running track. In field events, technique is as important as power and strength. In the high jump, for example, competitors must have perfect timing to transfer their running approach speed into jumping height. In the javelin throw, the winner is the person with the best throwing action. Jan Zelezny of the Czech Republic has perfected the javelin throw in the 1990s. His throw of 323 feet in 1996 remains an almost impossible target to beat. The javelin event derives from soldiers' spear-throwing contests at the ancient Olympics.

CARL LEWIS
Winner of 4 gold medals at the Los Angeles Olympics in 1984: the long jump, 100-meters, 200-meters, and 100-meter relay.

UP AND OVER
Before it became a sport, pole vaulting was an effective method for crossing ditches and fences.

The decathlon is an event where athletes compete over ten different track and field disciplines.

FACTS AND FIGURES

Overall, the U.S. has won more Olympic gold medals than any other country—833.

Romanian Lia Manoliu (36) won the discus throw in 1968—the oldest female Olympic winner.

Edwin Moses won 122 consecutive 400-meter hurdle races between 1977 and 1987.

Merlene Ottey, the Jamaican sprinter, has won a record 14 World Championship medals.

Maurice Greene ran the 100-meters in a record 9.79 seconds in Athens, June 16, 1999.

Bob Beamon's long jump world record, set in 1968, was not broken until 1991.

Tegla Loroupe of Kenya ran the women's marathon in a record 2h. 20m. 23s. in 1999.

FINE SHOT
China's Xinmei Sui won a silver medal in the shot put at the 1998 Olympics. The shot used to be a real cannon ball. The ancient Greeks used a heavy stone.

TEAM SPORTS

Many team sports began as unorganized games, with little thought of rules. Over time, as more people played the games, they evolved into the familiar sports we know today.

Bat and Ball

Sports involving a bat and ball have been played throughout history. There is even evidence to suggest that the ancient Greeks and Egyptians played a game with a ball and stick. The first game to evolve a set of fixed rules, with written copies dating back to 1744, is the game of cricket played in Britain. In the U.S., the most popular bat and ball game is baseball. The rules of baseball were developed by an amateur player, Alexander Cartwright, in 1845. Native Americans played their own bat and ball game, called baggataway, which prepared their young warriors for the trials of hunting.

BALL GAME
Cricket is one of the most popular games in England and in many countries that were once British colonies.

BASKETBALL
The tallest ever basketball player, at 8 ft., was Sulieman Ali Nashnush of Libya's 1962 national team.

The soccer World Cup trophy was stolen in 1966, but was later found under a bush.

Teamwork

Some team sports were developed to build fitness. In 1891, Dr. James Naismith, invented basketball in Springfield, Mass. as a means of making exercise more fun. His students enjoyed the game so much that news of it soon spread to other colleges. The National Basketball Association, the first professional basketball league, was formed in 1949. Although women's teams have existed nearly as long as men's, women's basketball did not receive professional recognition until 1996 when the U.S. women's Olympic team won the gold medal and the WNBA signed its first two players: Rebecca Lobo and Sheryl Swoopes.

ROW BOATS
Oxford and Cambridge, both universities in England, have competed in an annual boat race since 1829.

FACTS AND FIGURES

The Boston Celtics have won the most NBA basketball championships—16.

Harvard and Yale started the oldest annual collegiate regatta in the U.S. in 1852.

The most wins in a basketball season is 72, by the Chicago Bulls (1995–96).

In the first Superbowl, 1967, the Green Bay Packers beat the Kansas City Chiefs 35–10.

Two peach baskets and a soccer ball were used as the very first "baskets" and "ball."

Mia Hamm was soccer's Female Athlete of the Year five consecutive years (1994–98).

The New York Yankees have won the World Series a record 23 times.

DATABANK

Q Who was the greatest baseball all-rounder of all time?

A Babe Ruth set a record for home runs that wasn't broken for over 30 years.

Q Which country has won the soccer World Cup most often?

A Brazil has won the World Cup four times—in 1958, 1962, 1970, and 1994.

HOME RUN
Mark McGwire scored 70 home runs in the 1998 baseball season, narrowly beating Sammy Sosa to the record.

FALLEN HERO
Diego Maradona, a world famous soccer player for Argentina, was known for his speed, strength, and balance on the soccer field. But he was expelled from the 1994 World Cup for taking drugs.

LONG RUN
Desmond Howard of the Green Bay Packers won the MVP award at the 1997 Superbowl for running 99 yards—nearly a full field length—returning the kickoff.

Soccer

Soccer is one of the oldest sports in the world. Some believe that it originated in the Far East, where victorious soldiers would kick around the severed heads of defeated enemies. Today soccer is the world's most popular sport—millions of people in more than 140 countries throughout Europe and Latin America play soccer. Every four years, soccer's most famous international competition, the World Cup, is held. In 1991, the U.S. won the first women's World Cup. The team won again in 1999 in a penalty shoot out in front of 90,185 fans—a record attendance for a women's sport event.

Football

Derived from a mixture of the English games of rugby and soccer, football was played first in colleges before becoming a professional sport in 1920. The Superbowl, held annually between the season's two most successful teams, is one of the most popular television events of the year, watched by an average of 138 million people. First won in 1967 by the Green Bay Packers, the Superbowl has since been won a record five times each by the Dallas Cowboys and the San Francisco Forty-Niners.

Nolan Ryan, the world's fastest pitcher, can throw a baseball 100.9 mph.

SOLO SPORTS

In some sports, success depends on players working as a team. In others, it is up to the individual to find reserves of strength, courage, and skill to beat all opponents and set new personal goals.

WINNER
Although a U.K. competition, Wimbledon has not been won by a British man since Fred Perry's victory in 1936.

 ## Tennis

Tennis can be traced back to the French king's court in the 1100s. The modern game was adopted by the All-England Lawn Tennis and Croquet Club in 1877, when the Wimbledon tournament first took place. German Boris Becker became the youngest man to triumph at Wimbledon when he won the singles in 1987 at the age of 17. Great modern champions include Martina Navratilova and Pete Sampras with 8 and 6 singles titles respectively.

TRIUMPH
Germany's Steffi Graf won all four major tennis tournaments, known as the Grand Slam titles, in 1988.

Golf

Golf was played in Scotland as far back as the 1400s, but the first amateur championship was held in 1885. Today the four main golf titles for men are: the British Open, the U.S. Open, the PGA of America Championship, and the Masters Tournament—collectively know as the "Grand Slam." Golfing legend Jack Nicklaus is the only player to have won all four tournaments twice. Known as the "Golden Bear," Nicklaus won a total of 18 championships.

The sport of badminton is named after the Duke of Beaufort's house. He invented the game in 1873.

SWINGER
Eldrick "Tiger" Woods became the youngest person to win the Masters in 1997 at the age of 21. It is claimed that he swung his first golf club when he was just 11 months old.

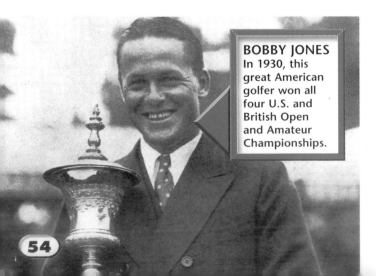

BOBBY JONES
In 1930, this great American golfer won all four U.S. and British Open and Amateur Championships.

DATABANK

Q What is the world's premier cycling competition?

A Established in 1903, the Tour de France brings together the world's best riders.

Q What age was the youngest Formula One motor racing champion?

A Brazilian Emerson Fittipaldi won the title at the age of 25 years and nine months in 1972.

FAST FERRARI
The successful Ferrari Formula One (or Grand Prix) team, won 125 Grand Prix victories by the end of the 1999 season.

 # Speed Masters

The first motor race was in France in 1894, shortly after the invention of the car. Early races were so dangerous that most were moved to special tracks. The average speed of the first races was 15 miles per hour, today cars reach speeds of over 150 miles per hour. The major titles are the Indy car series—the Indianapolis 500 is its highlight—and the World Driver's Championship raced over a season of 15 or 16 Grand Prix races.

IRON MIKE
Mike Tyson, shown here with the U.K.'s Frank Bruno, was one of the most feared boxers.

Fists of Fury

Boxing was one of the original sports at the Olympic games in ancient Greece. The Romans also used a form of boxing, but prohibited it around 100 B.C. In 1872, the Queensberry rules on which modern boxing is based, were adopted to make the sport safer. Muhammad Ali was one of the world's greatest and most charismatic boxers. After winning an Olympic title in 1960, Ali turned professional, becoming world heavyweight champion a record three times before retiring.

FACTS AND FIGURES

U.K. tennis player Greg Rusedski can hit a tennis ball at up to 148 mph.

The horse *Red Rum* won the Grand National, the famous steeplechase horse race, a record three times.

At 45, Hale Irwin became the oldest player to win the U.S. Open golf championship.

Argentina's Juan Manuel Fangio won the World Driver's Championship title five times.

Heavyweight boxer Rocky Marciano won all of his 49 professional fights.

Most boxers fight in categories that are determined by their weight—from flyweight to heavyweight.

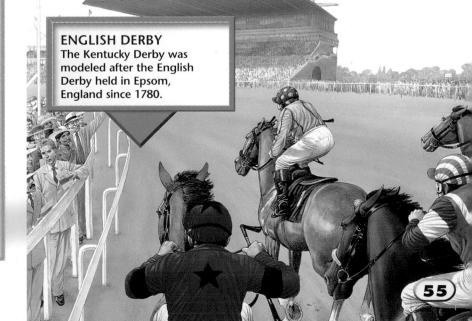

ENGLISH DERBY
The Kentucky Derby was modeled after the English Derby held in Epsom, England since 1780.

WINTER SPORTS

Sports competitions are not restricted to the summer months—even in the snow and ice, people still challenge each other to master the hostile winter conditions.

On the Slopes

The oldest skis have been found in Scandinavia and date back 5,000 years. These were not used for sports, but as a reliable form of transportation on snow.

The modern sport of skiing is split into two rival traditions. "Nordic" skiing includes cross-country skiing, biathlon, and ski-jumping while "alpine" skiing focuses on downhill and slalom events. In the men's Nordic events, Norwegian Bjørn Dæhlie reigns supreme, winning eight Olympic medals since 1992 and a further six World Cup titles. In alpine disciplines, Vreni Schneider of Switzerland won all seven women's World Cup slalom titles in the 1988–89 season. Austrian Franz Klammer has won five men's World Cup downhill titles, while Luxembourg's Marc Giradelli has equalled this achievement in a range of alpine events. Skiing is still evolving, with variations like snowboarding becoming popular.

A slope of compacted snow that is used to host skiing events is called the piste.

DATABANK

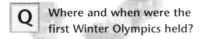

Q Where and when were the first Winter Olympics held?

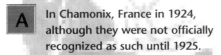

A In Chamonix, France in 1924, although they were not officially recognized as such until 1925.

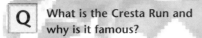

Q What is the Cresta Run and why is it famous?

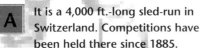

A It is a 4,000 ft.-long sled-run in Switzerland. Competitions have been held there since 1885.

OLYMPIAN
Jean-Luc Cretier of France won gold in the men's downhill event at the 1998 Winter Olympics in Nagano, Japan.

FACTS AND FIGURES

Germany's Katrina Witt won Olympic and World figure skating titles in 1984 and 1988.

The fastest speed reached by a skater is 154 mph by Austria's Harry Egger in 1999.

Australia beat New Zealand 58 – 0 in an ice hockey game in 1987—the most goals ever scored.

Ski binding inventor Sondre Nordheim won the first ski jump competition in 1866.

Georg Hackl of Germany has won a record six World Championship luge titles.

By the end of 1998, Karine Ruby of France had won 11 snowboarding world titles.

Ice Hockey

Played since the mid-1700s, ice hockey is a mixture of Native American games and the sport of field hockey. In Canada, where it is hugely popular, the sport was originally played outside, with the first indoor rink opening in 1875. Today, most teams have their own indoor venue. The Stanley Cup is awarded to the best team of the National Hockey League.

GIVING THEM STICK
Known as "The Great One," Canadian Wayne Gretzky scored 1,072 goals in his 20-year career.

With players moving at speeds of up to 31 mph, ice hockey is the fastest team sport in the world.

ICE BULLET
In the luge, competitors wear rubber suits to reduce wind resistance. They travel at up to 62 mph.

SKATES ON
A full Olympic sport since 1994, short-track speed skating requires great skill. Groups of skaters race each other at close quarters around a tight 364 ft. track.

Bobsledding

Winter sports involving a sled date from the 1500s. Bobsledding, where the competitors speed down an ice-covered slope on a specially designed sled emerged at the end of the 1800s. Taking its name from the bobbing movement of the riders—used to increase speed—the modern sport is divided into two- and four-man events. Switzerland is the premier bobsledding nation and has won the world four-man title 20 times.

CHEMISTRY

Chemistry is the study of what things are made from. This involves examining how elements and compounds behave and how they react with other substances.

Elements and Compounds

Everything is made up of a limited number of chemical elements. Scientists have discovered 109, and each has different properties. Yet 98 percent of the earth's crust is made up of only eight elements, including oxygen, iron, aluminum, sodium, and calcium. Elements combine to form new substances—called compounds—of which there are millions. Water is a compound of oxygen and hydrogen, while salt is a compound of sodium and chlorine.

BUCKYBALL
Buckyballs—or fullerenes—are the third form of pure carbon known to exist after graphite and diamond.

SOLID LIQUID?
The surface of a liquid acts like a stretchy skin. It is strong enough to hold very light things like this pond skater.

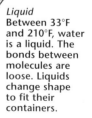

Altered States

Matter—anything that occupies space—exists in three states: gas, liquid, or solid. In solid objects, the molecules are bonded together tightly and cannot move. In liquids, the bonds are looser, so the molecules move freely against each other. In gases, the bonds are broken. There is nothing to stop the substance spreading out and filling the space it is in.

At room temperature, 2 elements are liquid, 96 are solids, and 11 are gases.

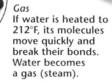

Gas
If water is heated to 212°F, its molecules move quickly and break their bonds. Water becomes a gas (steam).

Liquid
Between 33°F and 210°F, water is a liquid. The bonds between molecules are loose. Liquids change shape to fit their containers.

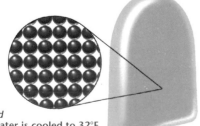

Solid
If water is cooled to 32°F or below, the molecules bond together tightly in a solid known as ice.

WEIRD WATER
Water has baffled scientists because as a solid (ice) it is less dense than when it is a liquid—unlike all other solids.

Helium melts at –457°F while carbon in the form of diamond melts at 6332°F.

90 percent of matter in the universe is hydrogen. It is also the lightest element.

The rarest natural element is astatine. Less than .017 oz. of this is present in earth's crust.

The first elements to be discovered were metals, used since prehistoric times.

The heaviest naturally occurring element is uranium. It is used in nuclear reactions.

The lightest metal is lithium. It weighs about half as much as water, so it floats!

When iron (a solid metal) is heated to over 2802°F, it becomes a liquid.

Water has two hydrogen atoms and one oxygen atom. Its chemical formula is H_2O.

Chemical Reactions

Chemical reactions occur all around us, creating new substances from existing ones. For example, water is created when hydrogen and oxygen are bonded together. When a chemical reaction occurs, the bonds between molecules break, enabling elements to combine with each other, forming compounds. Reactions are used to produce many items, including soap, medicines, cosmetics, paint, and plastic. Reactions even occur within our bodies. The oxygen that we breathe in reacts with glucose—a sugar compound containing hydrogen, carbon, and oxygen found in food— to produce energy, water, and a waste gas called carbon dioxide. We use up the energy and water and breathe out the carbon dioxide (a compound of carbon and oxygen). Heat speeds up a reaction. For example, if you hold an iron pan over a strong flame, rust will form more quickly than normal.

EVERYDAY CHEMISTRY
Cement is vital in building. The chemicals within it react with water, making it harden and stick objects together.

When iron is mixed with carbon, it becomes extra hard. The new substance is called steel.

CORROSION
When the metal iron reacts with the gas oxygen, iron oxide, or rust, is created. Usually the reaction is very slow.

DATABANK

INPUT

Q How many elements exist naturally and how many have been created artificially?

Q Who are alchemists and are they similar to chemists?

Q What is the Periodic Table of Elements?

Q Who was the first person to discover how chemical reactions worked?

OUTPUT

A There are 95 naturally occurring elements. 14 more have been created in laboratories.

A In the past, alchemists tried to turn ordinary metal into gold. Their experiments were the beginning of chemistry.

A The Periodic Table of Elements is an attempt to arrange the elements in order, according to atom size.

A Frenchman Antoine Lavoisier (1743–94) examined reactions by studying the role of oxygen in fire.

PHYSICS

Physics is the study of how the universe works. Physicists research everything from tiny things, such as atoms, to unbelievably large things, such as solar systems.

AIR FORCE
After being heated, air rises and pushes against the fabric of a balloon, pushing it upward against the pull of gravity.

Forces

A force is something that pushes or pulls an object in a particular direction. When you throw a ball or lift a weight, you exert a force on the object. The English scientist Isaac Newton (1642–1727) discovered that if an object exerts a force on another, it receives an equal and opposite force in return. For example, if you rollerskate up to a wall and push it, you move in the opposite direction—the wall "pushes" you back. But forces also keep things standing still. You might expect a car to roll down any slope—the force of gravity (see below) normally pulls it down. However, if the slope is only slight, another type of force between the car's tires and the slope stops it from moving. This force is called friction. The friction between the soles of your shoes and the floor enables you to grip the ground. Without it, you might slip and fall.

POTENTIAL
When a spring is pulled back, such as in pinball, it is ready to exert a force. It has what is called *potential energy*.

BOUNCER
A tennis ball falls because of gravity. As it hits the ground, it receives an equal force and bounces up.

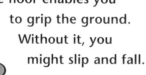

FACTS AND FIGURES

Electric current is measured in amps—after French physicist André Ampère (1775–1836).

Italian Alexandro Volta (1745–1827) made the first battery in 1800.

The first person to break up the nucleus of an atom was British physicist Ernest Rutherford in 1917.

The word atom comes from the Greek word *atomos*, which means "uncut."

An atom is thought to be about 0.00000001cm wide.

Friction is strongest between objects with rough surfaces.

SHAPED FOR FLIGHT
A wing is shaped so that air pressure is higher beneath it than above it. This sucks up the wing.

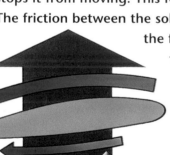

Gravity

Objects exert a force of attraction toward each other that is known as gravity. The larger the object's mass (the amount of matter it contains), the greater the attraction. Earth's mass is so huge, it pulls everything nearby toward it. The sun's gravity is even greater and keeps the planets in orbit around it. The moon's gravity pulls the water around in the oceans, causing tides.

BEATING GRAVITY
To stay in the air planes need the forces of lift and thrust to oppose the forces of gravity and drag.

Magnetism

Magnets attract materials containing iron, steel, or nickel and have two poles—north and south. The first law of magnetism is that like poles repel each other and opposite poles attract. All magnets are surrounded by a magnetic field. This area consists of invisible lines that go from the north to south poles of a magnet. Physicist Joseph Henry, (1797–1878) discovered that magnetic fields are closely related to electricity (see below).

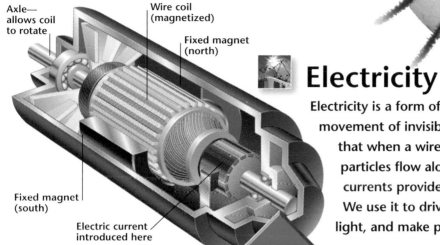

Axle—allows coil to rotate

Wire coil (magnetized)

Fixed magnet (north)

Fixed magnet (south)

Electric current introduced here

COMPASS
Earth is like a huge magnet, with a north and south pole. A compass contains a tiny magnet that is attracted to earth's north pole. This helps travelers find their way.

 # Electricity

Electricity is a form of energy produced by the movement of invisible particles. Henry noticed that when a wire is moved between two magnets, particles flow along the wire making an electrical current. These currents provide us with a versatile and clean form of energy. We use it to drive motors (left), produce light, and make powerful electromagnets.

ELECTRIC MOTOR
An electric current turns a wire coil into a magnet. Fixed magnets "repel" the coil and cause it to spin—creating a motor.

ATOM BOMB
An atom bomb splits billions of atom's nuclei at the same time, creating a chain reaction and a huge explosion.

 # Atoms

Atoms are the building blocks of the universe. Everything around us is made up of atoms. An atom has a center called a nucleus surrounded by particles called electrons. The nucleus is made up of particles called protons and neutrons. Scientists can split the nucleus of an atom. This starts off a chain reaction, which can release a vast amount of heat and energy— the basis for nuclear power.

INSIDE THE BOMB
This contains several pieces of radioactive material that react when brought together, causing their atoms to split.

NUCLEAR REACTOR
This power plant produces energy by splitting atoms. The energy drives generators, which produce electricity.

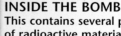

INVENTIONS

An invention is a new item or technique created by humans. Inventors take existing knowledge and use it in a different way. Many inventions have changed the way we live.

 ## Full Steam Ahead

Boiling water creates steam. Engineers realized that steam, when channeled, could be used as energy to drive a machine. In 1698, Englishman Thomas Savery designed an engine for pumping water—a design improved by Englishman Thomas Newcomen and, later, James Watt. Steam was then used to power locomotives and ships.

ROTARY STEAM ENGINE
Scotsman James Watt's rotary steam engine became a major source of power for industry, particularly in large factories.

 ## The Home

Joseph Henry discovered how to generate electricity in 1830, but it was years before it had a practical use in the home. By the early 1900s, inventors designed electrical appliances, such as electric washers, vacuum cleaners, and fans, which saved time and energy. Many people who had used servants to look after their houses now did their own chores.

IRON
Irons used to be heated over a fire. The first electric irons were dangerous. Safer versions arrived in 1882.

SQUEEZE DRY
The first washing machine was designed by James King in 1851. It was powered by hand.

FACTS AND FIGURES

Hero of Alexandria created a primitive steam engine in the 1st century A.D.

Christopher Sholes created the first efficient typewriter in 1868.

Englishman Sir John Harrington designed the first flushing toilet in 1596.

Thomas Edison held a world record 1,093 patents, either singly or jointly.

As well as inventing the telephone, Alexander Bell experimented with flight!

The first public telephone systems were in use by 1880.

A discovery, like electricity, is not an invention. It has always existed but was only "found" recently.

LIGHT BULB
Britain's Joseph Swan exhibited an electric light in 1860. He was followed 20 years later by Thomas Edison. The two men developed a practical light bulb in 1880.

 ## Telephone

Scotsman Alexander Graham Bell invented the telephone in 1876. His work with the deaf led him to examine how sound vibrates in the air. He found that electrical currents could be altered to resemble the vibrations of the voice. With his assistant, Thomas Watson, he built the "Box Telephone."

PHONE BOX
Bell's telephone converted the voice into an electrical current which could be sent along wires to a receiver.

Historical Buildings

The Egyptians, Greeks, and Romans built on an enormous scale. Some of their most famous buildings, such as the Acropolis in Athens, were erected in honor of the gods. During the Middle Ages and Renaissance, buildings in Europe were also dominated by religion.

St. Peter's in Rome, which was rebuilt in the 1500s, remained the world's largest Christian church until 1989, when it was surpassed by the basilica in Yamoussoukro on the Ivory Coast. Defense also influenced building in ancient times. The Great Wall of China, which is about 4,000 miles long, was built from 221 to 206 B.C. to protect China from invaders. If it was stretched out it would reach across the United States from New York to California.

DEFENSE
The art of castle building was at its height in the Middle Ages. The strongest castles had walls over 3 ft. thick. Rounded turrets at each corner gave defending archers a wide angle of fire.

LOPSIDED
The Leaning Tower of Pisa was built in 1174 on soft ground and has been tilting over ever since.

The Krak des Chevaliers was one of the most impenetrable castles ever built. Its ruins stand in modern Syria.

FACTS AND FIGURES

Built in A.D. 900, Ankhor Wat temple in Cambodia is the world's largest religious site.

The Egyptian Imhotep, who lived in about 2600 B.C., is history's first known architect.

Rome's Colosseum, completed in A.D. 80, could hold 50,000 spectators.

The Taj Mahal in India took 22 years to complete and needed up to 20,000 workers daily.

The Great Pyramid is 482 ft. high and is built from about 2.3 million blocks of stone.

The defensive walls of Great Zimbabwe in southern Africa were 33 ft. high and 16.4 ft. thick.

The Blue Mosque in Istanbul, built 1550–57, has 400 tiny domes.

DATABANK

INPUT

Q Where is Stonehenge and when was it completed?

Q What was Rome's Colosseum used for?

Q When was Westminster Abbey in London built?

Q When were the first ever huts or houses built?

OUTPUT

A It was built from 3000 to 1800 B.C., in Wiltshire, England.

A It was a stadium for bloody hand to hand combat.

A 1065. It was rebuilt in 1245 by King Henry II.

A About 35,000 years ago.

MARBLE MARVEL
India's most famous monument, the Taj Mahal, was built in 1632–1649 by a Mogul emperor as a tomb for his beloved wife.

MODERN BUILDING

The use of steel and concrete has made the sky the limit for the engineers of today, and gives architects greater freedom to experiment with unusual and breathtaking building designs.

EPCOT CENTER
At Disney World in Florida, construction engineers have designed a futuristic structure using a lattice-work of ultra-strong metal triangles. It looks like a massive golf ball!

Tallest Building

The first "skyscrapers" were built in Chicago during the 1880s because of rising land prices. It was in New York that the record breakers were built. In 1930, the Chrysler Building topped the Eiffel Tower at 1,046 feet, and then a year later the Empire State Building soared to 1,250 feet. Not until 1973 was it overtaken by the World Trade Center, which stands 1,368 feet tall.

EVER UPWARD
Since the 1970s, engineers have pushed ever upward—adding radio masts to achieve greater height.

Canary Wharf
800 ft.
U.K. 1991

Bank of China
1,033 ft.
Hong Kong 1988

Chrysler
Building
1,046 ft.
1930

John
Hancock
Center
1,125 ft.
1968

Empire
State
Building
1,250 ft.
1930

World Trade
Center
1,370 ft.
1973

Sears
Tower
1,453 ft.
1974

Petronas
Towers
1,482 ft.
Malaysia
1996

CN
Tower
1,815 ft.
Canada
1975

Bridges

The Romans were expert bridge builders and many of their aqueducts stand today. The Pont du Gard in France, built in A.D. 14, is 820 feet long. Since then, even longer bridges have been constructed. When it was built in 1981, the Humber suspension bridge in the U.K. became the longest of its kind in the world, spanning 4,652 feet. It uses taut cables of many strands of steel to hold up its tremendous weight.

TAKING THE STRAIN
The Golden Gate Bridge in San Francisco, California is a suspension bridge. Built in 1937, it is 4,200 ft. long.

FACTS AND FIGURES

The world's tallest radio mast is KTHI-TV's in Fargo, ND. It is 2,097 ft. high.

The world's longest bridge is the Pontchartrain Causeway in Lousiana. It is 24 miles long.

At 1,400 feet tall, Ekibastuz power plant in Kazakhstan has the world's tallest chimney.

The Petronas Towers in Malaysia are the world's tallest inhabited buildings.

HARD SHELL
The Sydney Opera House's roof "shells" are made from slabs of concrete covered with ceramic tiles.

Inspiration

In the 1950s, a competition was held to design a new art center for Sydney, Australia. It was won by Danish architect Jørn Urzon whose shell-like design was inspired by South American temples and the boats in Sydney Harbour. One of the seven wonders of the modern world, the Sydney Opera House was opened in 1973 and has attracted millions of visitors. Another innovative modern design is the Pompidou Center in Paris, opened in 1977. The building's pipes, ducts, elevators, and supporting elements are all on the outside of the building and are brightly colored, drawing attention to the remarkable structure. It is one of the most famous cultural centers in the world.

Built in 1989, the SkyDome stadium in Toronto, Canada, has the world's first fully retractable roof.

DATABANK

INPUT

Q What will be the world's tallest inhabited building by the year 2001?

Q How long is the longest tunnel in the world and when was it built?

Q Which cities in the world have the most skyscrapers over 500 ft. tall?

OUTPUT

A The Shanghai World Financial Center, in China, begun in 1997, will be 1,509 ft. high.

A The Seikan railroad tunnel in Japan is 33.4 miles long and was completed in 1988.

A New York has 140; Chicago 68; Hong Kong and Houston both have 36.

UNDESEA TRAVEL
Each of the Channel Tunnel's record-breaking twin rail tunnels is 31 miles long and has a diameter of 25 ft.

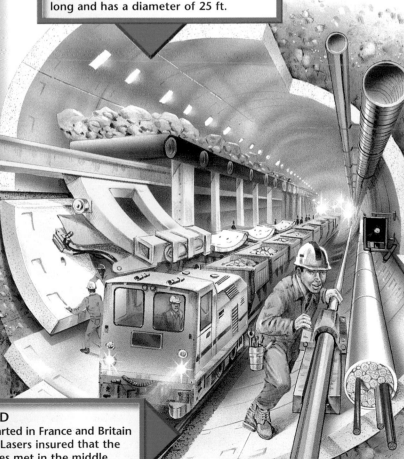

Channel Tunnel

A tunnel between England and France was planned over 200 years ago, but it was not until 1988 that it was started in earnest. Completed in 1994, the rail and service tunnels were dug by an Oahe-mole, a tungsten-tipped cutting machine. It moved a few yards per day lining the freshly excavated tunnels with concrete.

The first tunnel built under a navigable river was completed in 1843 under the River Thames in London.

LASER-GUIDED
Tunnels were started in France and Britain simultaneously. Lasers insured that the digging machines met in the middle.

ROAD AND RAIL

The wheel has been the most important technical innovation in human history. This simple device has been the basis for increasingly complicated modes of transportation—taking us farther and faster.

FIRST CARS
The first cars were powered by steam. They needed constant refueling and were slow and unreliable.

On Your Bicycle

The first commercially successful bicycle, the velocipede, was built in 1861 by Frenchman Pierre Michaux. The bicycle is an efficient and environmentally friendly form of transportation. With little effort, and no pollution, cyclists can cruise at 10–15 miles per hour—five times faster than walking.

Over 21 million Volkswagen Beetles have been sold since their launch in 1937.

THRUSTING
In 1983, *Thrust2*, driven by Richard Noble, set a 633 mph land-speed record at Black Rock Desert, NV.

The Highway

The first automobile with a gasoline engine was a three wheeler built by Karl Benz in 1885. It was followed by fellow German Gottlieb Daimler's four-wheeled "horseless carriage" in 1886. Early cars were expensive and it was not until Oldsmobile introduced mass production in the U.S. around 1904 that they dropped in price. Later, Henry Ford installed moving assembly lines to increase production even more. His Model T was designed as "the family horse" and by 1920 accounted for around half the cars sold. Since then, the car has become the world's most popular form of transportation.

In 1996, *Dream Solar*, a solar-powered car, covered 1,866 miles in 33.3 hours, averaging 53 mph.

FREIGHT TRAIN
Australia is vast and lacks an extensive rail network. Instead, goods are transported by trucks that pull long trains of trailers.

DATABANK

Q What is the fastest public passenger train?

A The Japanese "bullet train," which travels at an average speed of 162 mph.

Q Where did the penny-farthing bicycle get its name from?

A Its wheels resembled the old British penny and farthing coins.

GO WEST
Before the U.S. rail network was built, colonists moving west in search of new lands traveled in long convoys. These giant "wagon trains" made the hazardous journeys safer.

On Track

The first steam railroad engine was invented by Richard Trevithick in 1804. Intended as cheap industrial transportation, his engine carried 70 people and 10 tons of iron. In 1825, George Stephenson developed an engine to carry people on the first public railroad in the U.K. His *Rocket* had won the Rainhill trials, a national contest to find a reliable steam train for passenger travel. During the 1800s, steam railroads spread throughout Europe and the U.S., with hundreds of new lines opening every year. In the 1900s, railroad developers began searching for faster and more efficient alternatives to steam power. By 1939, electric locomotives designed to work over a range of slopes and other difficult conditions were built in the U.S., sealing the fate of steam power. Today, high-speed trains, like France's TGV, have become the standard. In 1990, a modified TGV set a record speed of 318 miles per hour. Despite this success, rail travel is in decline worldwide, as more people switch to car and air travel.

GREAT TRAIN
Der Adler was Germany's first steam railway engine. It was built by George Stephenson's son Robert in 1835.

FACTS AND FIGURES

The car *Thrust SSC* broke the land speed record in 1997, traveling at 761 mph.

In 1938, *Mallard* became the world's fastest steam train, reaching speeds of 125 mph.

The U.S. has over 4 million miles of roads and highways—more than any other country.

The Ford Mustang, introduced in 1964, was the first sports car in the U.S.

London has the oldest subway in the world. It opened in 1863.

MAGNETICS
The latest high tech trains use high powered electromagnets to float above special tracks. In tests in Germany, these futuristic trains have reached speeds of 270 mph.

BOATS

The first primitive boats were made from fallen trees. Since then people have built bigger and better ships in order to cross rivers, seas, and oceans to reach new lands.

 ## Sailing By

Ancient stone tablets suggest that people built boats as early as 4000 B.C. The funeral barge of the Egyptian emperor Cheops, the earliest ship to be discovered, dates back to about 3000 B.C. Early Egyptian boats were powered almost entirely by oarsmen, with the later addition of a single square sail to harness wind power. The Arabs, using ships called *boums*, were the masters of wind power. They used lateen (triangle-shaped) sails that could be adjusted to make the most of any available wind. By the 1400s, European ships carried a combination of square and lateen sails, allowing them to trade with the faraway lands of China and Southeast Asia. As sea trade increased, so did fierce competition between seagoing nations. Many ships had to be armed with cannon for protection and this led to specially built warships and large navies.

Built in 1797, the warship USS *Constitution* survived many battles and is preserved to this day.

FACTS AND FIGURES

Ken Warby reached 317 mph on water in the hydroplane *Spirit of Australia* in 1978.

The first passenger-carrying liners operated across the Atlantic Ocean in the 1840s.

Ancient Greek trireme galleys used three rows of oarsmen to increase speed.

HMS *Victory*, moored in Portsmouth, U.K., is the last ship of the line on earth.

Up to 7,800 people died when German liner *Wilhelm Gustloff* was torpedoed in 1945.

The first nuclear powered submarine, the *Nautilus*, was launched in 1954.

TEA CLIPPER
Clippers were used to transport cargo quickly. One, the *Lightning*, had 13,043 sq. yds. of sails, which, in 1854, enabled it to travel from Australia to the U.K. in a record 64 days.

In 1922, the first aircraft carrier in the U.S. navy was used—it was a converted coal carrier.

MERCHANT SHIPS
The prosperity of ancient Roman cities depended on trade ships to transport food, goods, and armies to other ports.

NATIVE BOAT
The Dzelarhon Native Americans used long and narrow vessels that were fast and easy to maneuver.

The nuclear-powered aircraft carrier, USS *Nimitz*, can sail around the world without refueling.

 # Warships

By 1800, naval battles centered on ships of the line, so called because they would line up alongside an enemy and fire as many cannons as possible into them. One such ship held 100 cannons and could hit ships 1,640 feet away. In 1906, the British navy unveiled the *Dreadnought*, a metal-hulled warship with guns that had a range of 9.3 miles. By the late 1900s, aircraft carriers and submarines carrying nuclear bombs had become the most important warships.

SUPER SUBMARINE
Modern submarines are nuclear-powered and operate undetected at sea for many months at a time.

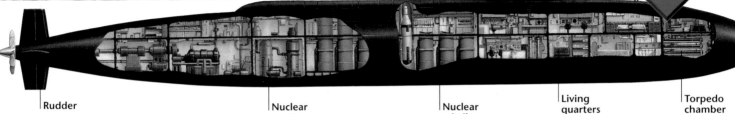

Rudder | Nuclear reactor | Nuclear missiles | Living quarters | Torpedo chamber

 # Cargo Carriers

Today, shipping is still the cheapest way to transport many goods around the world. Liquids such as oil are often transported in tankers—ships that get their name from the large tanks in which they carry their cargo. Other goods are carried on Roll-on/roll-off ships. These vessels have openings, or ports, at both ends of the ship that allow vehicles to drive on and off when moving goods. The *Jahre Viking* is the largest cargo vessel in the world. It carries over 300,000 tons.

LEVIATHAN
Tankers are the biggest ships. The largest tankers can displace over 250,000 tons of water when full.

DATABANK

Q What was the largest sailing ship in the world and what happened to it?

A The *France II* was 417 ft. long and had five masts. Launched in 1911, it was wrecked in 1922.

Q What was the biggest naval battle ever fought and who was involved?

A In 1916, 101 German and 151 British warships fought the Battle of Jutland in the North Sea.

Fishing boats catch over 1 billion tons of fish worldwide each year.

Weird Ships

The idea that a ship could float on a cushion of air dates from 1877, but it was Christopher Cockerell, a British engineer, who patented the first practical hovercraft design in 1955. *SR-N1*, based on Cockerell's designs, was built four years later. The hydrofoil, first built in Italy by Enrico Forlanini in 1900, also appears to float above the sea. In reality, it has long, winglike fins that force the ship upward when traveling at high speeds.

IN THE AIR
The biggest hovercraft in the world, the *SR.N4 MkIII*, weighs 310 tons and is more than 56m long.

FLIGHT

Humans have long envied birds. The first attempts to imitate them were simple and unreliable, but today's planes have mastered the air.

 ## Pioneers

In 1783, Joseph and Étienne Montgolfier of France launched the first human-piloted balloon, proving that people had the ability to defy gravity. Just over one hundred years later, Otto Lilienthal developed a primitive glider. In the U.S., Orville and Wilbur Wright, encouraged by the newly invented gasoline engine, built the first powered airplane, the *Flyer*. In 1903, this fragile two-wing plane flew just 120 feet, but it changed human history. By 1909, Frenchman Louis Blériot had built a plane powerful enough to fly the English Channel.

Balloons are filled with gas or hot air, which is much lighter than the surrounding air, so the balloon floats.

BIRD MAN
German inventor Otto Lilienthal studied flying birds in order to design his gliders. He crashed to his death in 1896.

Cockpit

Cargo hold

STEALTHY DOES IT
The American F-117 "stealth" fighter is designed to be undetectable by enemy radar so it can bomb targets safely.

 ## Warplanes

The first airplanes were powered by propellers. They evolved quickly during World War I (1914–18) as each side built faster and more agile fighters to control the skies. World War II (1939–45) sped up the development of jets, but the most crucial air battles were won by propeller-driven planes, such as the Spitfire, with its maximum speed of 440 miles per hour. Today most warplanes are jet-powered and some travel faster than the speed of sound— about 740 miles per hour.

RED BARON
The triplane's three wings made it very maneuverable during World War I air battles. It was favored by Baron Manfred Von Richthoven of Germany, the war's finest pilot.

The Harrier jump jet uses its jets to rise straight up on take off and does not need a runway.

FACTS AND FIGURES

Spanish engineer, Juan de la Cierva, built the autogyro (the first helicopter) in 1923.

The first transatlantic flight took place in 1919 from Newfoundland to Portugal.

British engineer Frank Whittle designed the first jet engine in 1937.

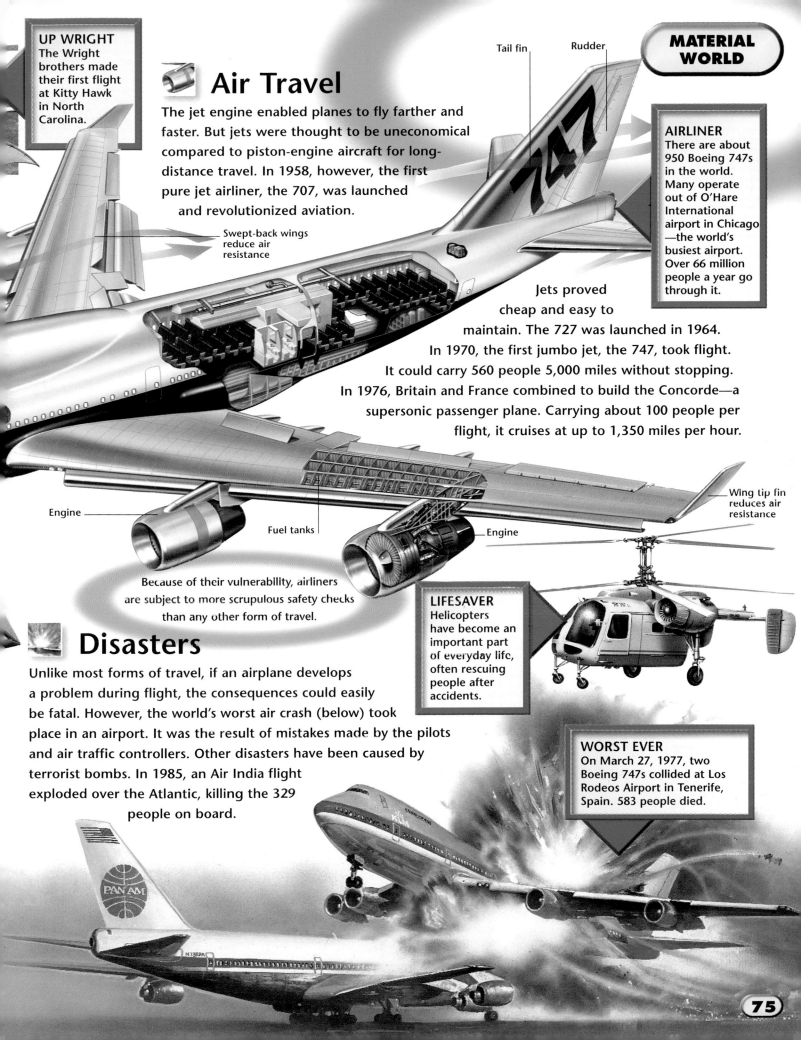

UP WRIGHT
The Wright brothers made their first flight at Kitty Hawk in North Carolina.

Tail fin

Rudder

Air Travel

The jet engine enabled planes to fly farther and faster. But jets were thought to be uneconomical compared to piston-engine aircraft for long-distance travel. In 1958, however, the first pure jet airliner, the 707, was launched and revolutionized aviation.

AIRLINER
There are about 950 Boeing 747s in the world. Many operate out of O'Hare International airport in Chicago —the world's busiest airport. Over 66 million people a year go through it.

Swept-back wings reduce air resistance

Jets proved cheap and easy to maintain. The 727 was launched in 1964. In 1970, the first jumbo jet, the 747, took flight. It could carry 560 people 5,000 miles without stopping. In 1976, Britain and France combined to build the Concorde—a supersonic passenger plane. Carrying about 100 people per flight, it cruises at up to 1,350 miles per hour.

Engine

Fuel tanks

Engine

Wing tip fin reduces air resistance

Because of their vulnerability, airliners are subject to more scrupulous safety checks than any other form of travel.

Disasters

Unlike most forms of travel, if an airplane develops a problem during flight, the consequences could easily be fatal. However, the world's worst air crash (below) took place in an airport. It was the result of mistakes made by the pilots and air traffic controllers. Other disasters have been caused by terrorist bombs. In 1985, an Air India flight exploded over the Atlantic, killing the 329 people on board.

LIFESAVER
Helicopters have become an important part of everyday life, often rescuing people after accidents.

WORST EVER
On March 27, 1977, two Boeing 747s collided at Los Rodeos Airport in Tenerife, Spain. 583 people died.

PAN AM

WEALTH AND RICHES

Money developed in early times as a more efficient way of trading goods and services than the simple act of swapping goods. Since then, it has become an important symbol of wealth, power, prestige, and influence.

 ## Money

In the ancient world, people traded one thing for another in a system known as barter, but there was no standard agreement on how much things were worth. Useful items, such as salt and daggers, became measures of value—as were ornamental objects, such as beads and seashells. The first coins, made from silver and gold, date from the reign of King Croesus of Lydia (now part of present-day Turkey), around 650 B.C. Coins were popular because they were durable and easy to carry. Soon, city states all over nearby Greece were making their own coins.

MILITARY MONEY
By 1 B.C., campaigning Roman generals had begun to make their own coins in order to pay their soldiers in the field.

WORTHLESS
After defeat in World War I, Germany was forced to print so much money that its currency became worthless. By November 1923, a loaf of bread cost over 200 billion marks.

The study of coins is called numismatics, and coin collectors are known as numismatists.

 ## Richest Countries

Countries measure their wealth in terms of Gross Domestic Product (GDP) per person. This is the value of all the goods and services produced within a country's borders each year, divided by its population. According to a 1997 United Nations survey, Luxembourg has the highest GDP at $37,785 per person. The lowest belongs to the Democratic Republic of Congo, which has a GDP of just $52 per person—over 726 times less than that of Luxembourg.

RICH DESERTS
Once very poor, Saudi Arabia became rich after the exploitation of its numerous oil reserves.

The Bank of England was founded in 1694 for the sole purpose of raising money for wars.

TRADE CENTER
After the devastating stock market crash of 1929, the New York Stock Exchange recovered to become one of the world's most important financial centers.

DATABANK INPUT

Q What is the biggest gambling win ever seen and where did it take place?

Q Which country produces the most gold in the world and how much does it produce?

Q What is the euro, who uses it, and when was it introduced?

Q What and where is Fort Knox—and why is it famous?

Superrich

The richest man in the world is probably Bill Gates who, in 1999, was estimated to be worth as much as $90 billion. Gates's wealth is based on the software company Microsoft, which he started in 1975. He is now richer than the Sultan of Brunei, an oil and gas magnate who was previously the world's wealthiest man. One of the superrich of the 1800s was John Davison Rockefeller, an oil tycoon who founded the Standard Oil Company in 1870. His company gave him control of the U.S. oil trade—and earned him a vast amount of money. Rockefeller became a great philanthropist, giving over $500 million to charity before his death in 1937. His personal fortune, estimated at $1.4 billion, was inherited by his son, John D. Rockefeller, Jr.

The richest person in the ancient world was Croesus of Lydia. His wealth was the source of legends.

FACTS AND FIGURES

There are over 8.7 billion one-dollar bills in circulation in the U.S.

Bill Gates became the youngest billionaire ever at the age of 31.

At the tender age of three, Athina Roussel inherited a $5 billion business empire.

Bahrain and Qatar, in the Persian Gulf, are so rich that they have a zero percent income tax rate.

Warren Buffet is the richest stock market trader, with a fortune of over $15 billion.

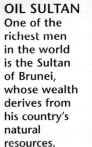

OIL SULTAN
One of the richest men in the world is the Sultan of Brunei, whose wealth derives from his country's natural resources.

RICH ROYALTY
The Queen of England's personal fortune of $720 million does not include the crown jewels or the land that comes with her title.

BILLIONAIRE
Bill Gates first started programming computers at the age of 13 and left Harvard University to found his own company. Today, his wealth is greater than that of many countries.

OUTPUT

A Two lucky winners from Wisconsin, won over $110 million on the Powerball Lottery in 1993.

A South Africa, which produced nearly 500 tons of gold in 1996, is the largest gold producer in the world.

A Adopted in 1999, the euro is the common currency for members of the European Union.

A Fort Knox is an army base in Kentucky famed for housing the U.S. gold reserve.

PRECIOUS OBJECTS

Diamonds and finely crafted gold jewelry are valued for their beauty, and other objects are precious because they are rare, strange, or have a religious significance. Each culture places value on different items.

FACTS AND FIGURES

A blue diamond ring was sold for $7.5 million in 1995—the most expensive ever.

A pair of gloves worn by the king of boxing, Muhammad Ali, sold for about $30,000.

A Japanese businessman paid $100,000 for a rare teddy bear in 1998.

In 1994, robbers in Cannes, France, stole $36 million worth of jewelry.

About 150 works by Picasso have sold for over $1.62 million each.

Gems and Jewels

Gems, such as diamonds and rubies, occur naturally and are valued for their rarity and beauty. The largest diamond found was the *Cullinan*. It measured 4 x 2 x 2 inches. Presented to Britain's King Edward VII, it was cut into smaller gems, which now adorn the British crown jewels. Pearls, made by humble oysters, are also greatly treasured.

Jewelers cut large natural diamonds into smaller stones to improve their quality.

TOP HAT
Crown jewels symbolized a monarch's power. They were worn to impress subjects and enemies.

Buried treasure

In the 1870s, while excavating Troy in Turkey, German Heinrich Schliemann found a great treasure hoard. He identified it as belonging to Troy's legendary king, Priam. The Dead Sea Scrolls were found in Israel in 1947. One famous treasure has yet to be found—the Holy Grail. It is said to be the cup used by Jesus at the Last Supper.

RESCUED FROM THE DEPTHS
Objects recovered from shipwrecks, like the English *Mary Rose* that sank in 1545, help historians to understand the past.

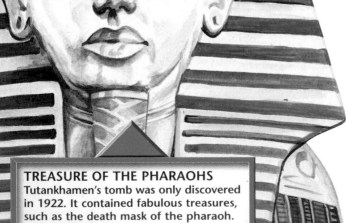
TREASURE OF THE PHARAOHS
Tutankhamen's tomb was only discovered in 1922. It contained fabulous treasures, such as the death mask of the pharaoh.

DATABANK

INPUT	OUTPUT
Q What is the hardest gemstone in the world?	**A** Diamonds are the hardest naturally occurring substance on earth.
Q What happens if I find some old jewelry lying in a field? May I keep it?	**A** In some countries, a treasure without a known owner becomes state property.
Q Why are people prepared to pay so much for old pictures or antiques?	**A** Collectors are usually attracted by an object's age, rarity, and unique qualities.

Collectables

Works by respected artists, such as Fabergé, Picasso, and Van Gogh, are guaranteed to sell for many millions of dollars. Some objects are valuable for less obvious reasons. Rare children's toys, such as early teddy bears, are eagerly sought. In 1994, a collector paid over $20,000 for a toy truck that was made in 1937. A famous person's belongings may also be valuable. President John F. Kennedy's comb was sold for over $1,000, while the birth certificate of famous singer Paul McCartney fetched $84,146.

Russian jeweler, Karl Fabergé, created beautiful eggs from precious metals and gems for Russian rulers.

RARE STAMP
Old and unusual stamps, such as England's Penny Black—the first ever stamp—are highly prized by collectors.

SUNFLOWERS
Van Gogh's *Sunflowers* was auctioned for $36.5 million in1987. But rumors suggest that it is a fake.

HEADS
Coins were once made from precious metals. Today, such coins are worth far more than their face value.

TOMB RAIDER
Many treasures of ancient Egypt were stolen by grave robbers. Gold statues were melted down and sold.

Theft and Thieves

Wherever there are precious objects, there will be people aiming to steal them. The fabled Amber Room of the Catherine Palace in Russia was removed by German soldiers on Hitler's orders in 1945 and has vanished. A single panel mysteriously reappeared in 1997. Edvard Munch's famous painting *The Scream* was stolen from Norway's National Art Gallery in 1994. Luckily, it was soon recovered.

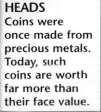

VIKING RAID
In the past, in times of war, people often hid or buried their valuables. Such hoards are still being uncovered today.

ART

Works of art are how artists honestly interpret what they see or feel. Art can take many different forms, including painting and sculpture.

 ## Early Art

The ancient Greeks were the first to see art as a pleasure rather than as an homage to the gods. But early European art used religious images in Biblical illustrations (above), such as the *Lindisfarne Gospels* (A.D. 700). In Islamic works, human images were taboo, but abstract art flourished. It reached its peak in the building of the Alhambra Palace in Granada, Spain, 1338–90. Because of its beauty Christian monarchs did not destroy it!

ILLUSTRATED MANUSCRIPT
In medieval art, the religious message was more important than the accuracy of the figures in the painting.

FACTS AND FIGURES

Masaccio's *Holy Trinity*, painted in 1427, is the first example of perspective in art.

A set of 356 cone sculptures, called *Desert Breath*, covers 25 acres of Egypt's desert.

Made in 1080 in Normandy, the hand-stitched Bayeux Tapestry is 230 ft. long.

The Postimpressionist artist Paul Cézanne is regarded as the founder of modern art.

Thousands of paintings have vanished without a trace—including 350 by Picasso.

The earliest examples of art are cave paintings from about 40,000 years ago.

 ## Renaissance

Renaissance means "rebirth" and refers to the period from 1350 to 1550 when Italian artists tried to revive the glory of ancient Greek and Roman art. Artists such as Botticelli, Raphael, and Da Vinci took art to a higher plane, using perspective and depth to add realism to their art. One of the most celebrated artists of the age was Michelangelo. He was master of the human form, as is shown in his sculpture *David* and the painting *The Creation of Adam* (below). He was also an architect.

Renaissance artists succeeded in making their subjects look natural— a revolution at that time!

MICHELANGELO'S MASTERPIECE
Michelangelo frescos, painted from 1508 to 1512 on the ceiling of the Sistine Chapel, Rome, are among his best works.

Impressionism

Toward the end of the 1800s, some French artists evolved a new style of painting. Artists like Manet, Monet, and Seurat wanted to portray life in a fresh way, conveying an "impression" of a scene rather than painting it in detail. They experimented widely with light, color, and texture. Their work influenced artists all over the world, who began to paint in a freer, livelier way.

The Impressionists were followed by the Post-impressionists, who wanted to give art more solidity.

SUNDAY AFTERNOON
Georges Seurat (1859–91) built up his pictures from tiny dots of paint. His style gives an "impression" of a scene.

Modern art

The Impressionists' new approach led many artists to reject the ideas of the past. Instead of showing life as we see it, they became more and more experimental. Vincent Van Gogh (1853–90) used color and form to convey what he felt about the things he painted. Pablo Picasso (1881–1973) tested how far he could go in painting abstract images of everyday objects. Piet Mondrian (1872–1944) built pictures out of straight lines and colors. Such ideas consistently scandalized the art critics of their time. Even today challenging works by leading artists, such as Damian Hirst, draw as much criticism as they do praise.

In 1991, Damian Hirst held an exhibition that included an entire dead shark preserved in a tank.

POP ART
Andy Warhol (1926–87) was the pioneer of pop art, which linked art and popular culture, by painting cola bottles and soup cans. He filmed over 6,000 hours of his own life.

DATABANK

Q What is considered to be the most valuable painting in the world?

A *Mona Lisa* (1502) by da Vinci. It is considered priceless but in 1963 was valued at £35 million.

Q What are Europe's most famous art museums and where are they?

A They include the Louvre, Paris, France; the Uffizi, Florence, Italy; and the Prado, Madrid, Spain.

THE WRITTEN WORD

The first stories were recounted orally, but with the invention of writing and, later, printing, the written word became a universal means of sharing ideas.

  ## Printing

Before printing, books had to be copied by hand—so few were made. The Chinese first used printed type in the 1000s, but it was another 400 years before the technique appeared in Europe. By the 1700s, presses could print 1,000 pages an hour; newspapers and books became available to everyone.

In 1517, Martin Luther used mass-produced leaflets to spread his rebellion against the Church.

One of the earliest novels is *The Tale of Genji* written by Japan's Lady Murasaki Shikibu in the 1000s.

THE PRINTING PRESS
German Johann Gutenberg invented the printing press in 1455. It allowed exact copies to be made of text and images.

DOMESDAY BOOK
William the Conqueror's painstaking survey of England in 1086 is one of history's greatest surviving records.

FACTS AND FIGURES

The Library of Congress in Washington, D.C. holds over 23 million books.

The oldest handwritten copy of the Koran dates from A.D. 1091 from Bangladesh.

The novelist George Eliot (1819–80) was really a woman named Mary Ann Evans.

The great poem *The Epic of Gilgamesh*, from Sumeria (Turkey), dates from 2000 B.C.

Pencils date from the 1490s. Hungarian Laslo Biro invented the ballpoint pen in 1938.

 ## Books for Kids

It was once thought that children's books should offer only stern moral lessons. By the 1800s, however, Mark Twain's *Adventures of Tom Sawyer* (1876) and Rudyard Kipling's *The Jungle Book* (1894) offered more exciting reading. The first modern picture book was Beatrix Potter's *Tale of Peter Rabbit* (1900). It was followed by A. A. Milne's *Winnie the Pooh* in 1926, enhanced with illustrations by Ernest Shepherd. Today, the *Harry Potter* novels by British author J. K. Rowling are a great favorite with children around the world.

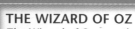

THE WIZARD OF OZ
The Wizard of Oz was the first of 14 books about the magical world of Oz by L. Frank Baum.

J.K. ROWLING
HARRY POTTER

JUNIOR WIZARD
After discovering that he is a wizard, Harry Potter goes to Hogwarts wizard school where he has many adventures.

Drama

Before television and film, theater provided public entertainment. In the Middle Ages, plays had religious themes, but in the late 1500s the subject matter broadened. In Britain, William Shakespeare and others wrote comedies and tragedies to capture public imagination.

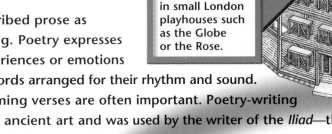
Great modern playwrights include Russia's Anton Checkov, and Ireland's Sean O'Casey and Samuel Beckett.

THE BARD
Shakespeare's plays used to be performed in small London playhouses such as the Globe or the Rose.

Poetry

French poet Paul Valéry described prose as walking and poetry as dancing. Poetry expresses experiences or emotions in words arranged for their rhythm and sound. Rhyming verses are often important. Poetry-writing is an ancient art and was used by the writer of the *Iliad*—the epic of the Trojan War (800–700 B.C.). Modern poets use poetry to decribe anything from heaven and hell to the health of a pet goldfish.

Novels

A novel explores life using characters and a story line. Novels gained popularity in the 1700s and 1800s through the works of Victor Hugo, Leo Tolstoy, Charles Dickens, and Louisa May Alcott. There are many types of novels. Raymond Chandler and Agatha Christie wrote about crime, Isaac Asimov is famous for science fiction, while J. R. R. Tolkien's *Lord of the Rings* is an epic fantasy fairy tale.

CERVANTES
The Spanish writer Miguel de Cervantes wrote *Don Quixote* in 1605—one of the first novels. It follows the adventures of the hapless hero who wants to be a chivalrous knight of old.

Comic Books

A comic is a series of pictures and words that tell a story. Early comics got their name from the funny stories they told. Comic books became popular with the creation of the superhero *Superman* in the 1930s. Many early comics like the *Spiderman* and *Batman* are still popular with children today.

Tintin is one of the most famous comic characters. He was created by the Belgian Hergé in 1929.

LEGENDARY DARK KNIGHT
Created by Bob Kane, the popular character Batman first appeared in *Detective Comics* 27 in May 1939.

MUSIC

From simple, prehistoric drums to the computerized dance tunes of the 1990s, music has played a vital part in almost every human culture.

In John Cage's *4'33"*, the performers sit in silence and the "music" is any noise made by the audience.

Early Music

Pipes and drums have been found among the remains of the earliest settlements. Drums and string instruments, such as the harp, may have evolved from beating cooking pots and twanging the strings of hunting bows. The ancient Egyptians, Chinese, Romans, and Greeks were all sophisticated singers and musicians, but the earliest piece of music found to date is a hymn from Sumeria (present-day Iraq) from about 700 B.C.

SOUND OF THE SOUTH
Invented by Australian aborigines, the didgeridoo is a wind instrument that has a unique, haunting tone.

Despite his fame and talent, Mozart died penniless at the age of 35 and was buried in an unmarked grave.

Classical Music

Classical and baroque music began in the Middle Ages in Italy, so most musical terms are Italian. Yet music was taken to greater heights by German composers such as Johann Sebastian Bach (1685–1750)—regarded by many as the most accomplished musician ever. The child prodigy, Wolfgang Amadeus Mozart (1756–91), further developed musical styles, writing 27 piano concertos. Ludwig van Beethoven (1770–1827) pioneered the "romantic" style, which continues to influence classical music today. The 1900s saw the rise of recorded music—bringing classical music into the home.

PIANOFORTE
The piano was invented in Italy in 1709. Its full name describes how it plays notes both loudly and softly.

YOU WHAT?
Although he did not become totally deaf until 1819, Beethoven wrote much of his music, including his famous *Fifth Symphony*, while his hearing was severely impaired.

FACTS AND FIGURES

Candle in the Wind by Elton John, with sales of 35 million, is the best-selling single ever.

The earliest organ, the ancient greek hydraulus, dates from about 230 B.C.

Wolfgang Amadeus Mozart wrote 200 musical works by the age of 18.

Stevie Wonder was only 13 years old when his debut album went to the top of the U.S. charts.

In 1994, 3.5 million people saw Rod Stewart's concert in Rio de Janeiro, Brazil.

The most successful boy band in the world so far is New Kids on the Block.

DATABANK

INPUT

Q Which musical instruments are known as woodwind instruments?

Q What is opera and where did it originate?

Q Who was the first rock and roll singer or band—and what was their first song?

Q What is soul music and who are the greatest soul singers?

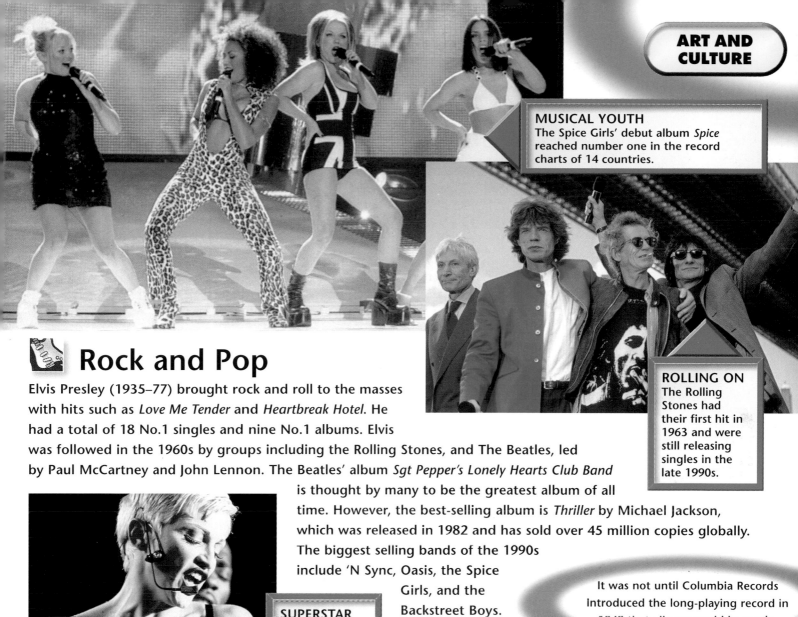

MUSICAL YOUTH
The Spice Girls' debut album *Spice* reached number one in the record charts of 14 countries.

ROLLING ON
The Rolling Stones had their first hit in 1963 and were still releasing singles in the late 1990s.

Rock and Pop

Elvis Presley (1935–77) brought rock and roll to the masses with hits such as *Love Me Tender* and *Heartbreak Hotel*. He had a total of 18 No.1 singles and nine No.1 albums. Elvis was followed in the 1960s by groups including the Rolling Stones, and The Beatles, led by Paul McCartney and John Lennon. The Beatles' album *Sgt Pepper's Lonely Hearts Club Band* is thought by many to be the greatest album of all time. However, the best-selling album is *Thriller* by Michael Jackson, which was released in 1982 and has sold over 45 million copies globally. The biggest selling bands of the 1990s include 'N Sync, Oasis, the Spice Girls, and the Backstreet Boys.

It was not until Columbia Records Introduced the long-playing record in 1948 that albums could be made.

SUPERSTAR
Madonna's first major album released in 1983 included five U.S. hit singles.

OUTPUT

A — The flute, oboe, piccolo, clarinet, bassoon, and recorder are woodwind instruments.

A — Opera could be described as theater and poetry set to music. It originated in Italy in the 1600s.

A — Bill Haley and His Comets are regarded as the first. Their first single, *Rock Around the Clock,* was released in 1955.

A — Soul grew out of African–American gospel music. Singers include Aretha Franklin and James Brown.

Jazz and Blues

Jazz is a blend of African musical traditions and European folk and classical styles. It first emerged at the end of the 1800s among the marching bands in southern U.S. cities such as New Orleans. Two of the greatest jazz musicians were Louis Armstrong and Duke Ellington. Blues also evolved in the South. Its roots lie in West African music and work songs.

THAT'S JAZZ
Jazz was the "pop" music of the first half of the 1900s. Jazz clubs are still extremely popular today.

CINEMA

The major art form of the 1900s, moving pictures (or "movies") are made primarily to entertain audiences, but are also a record of our ever-changing world.

SCREEN IDOL
Greta Garbo (1905–90) was a great star of silent films and talkies. She lived as a recluse from 1941 onward.

Silent Era

The first filmmakers experimented with sound, but films were silent until 1927. One of the earliest films, *The Great Train Robbery* (1903), was also the first western. It lasted just ten minutes. Big studios relied on major stars, such as Mary Pickford, to bring in audiences. The most famous of all was comic Charlie Chaplin.

In 1896, *The Kiss Between May Irvin and John C. Rice* showed cinema's first screen kiss.

TALKIE TIME
The first film with sound was *The Jazz Singer* (1927), starring Al Jolson. It was also the first musical.

Hollywood

The home of the film industry, Hollywood's legend began when a group of movie producers moved there just before World War I. The studios they founded, including Twentieth Century Fox and Metro-Goldwyn-Mayer (MGM), controlled moviemaking by the 1930s, and turned it into the multimillion-dollar business it still is today.

SOME LIKE IT HOT
Marilyn Monroe (1926–62) was, for many, the ultimate Hollywood icon. She died of an overdose of sleeping pills.

LIGHTS! CAMERA! ACTION!
Film producers and directors originally moved to Hollywood because of the pleasant climate and wide-open spaces.

FACTS AND FIGURES

In 1895, the Lumière brothers were the first to show films to paying customers.

Titanic (1997), is the most expensive film ever made. It cost $2 billion.

Ben-Hur (silent, 1925) cost $4 million to make. The 1959 remake cost $14.5 million.

Over 300 films have been made worldwide of William Shakespeare's plays.

India produces more films than any other country—with a peak of 948 films in 1990.

The longest film of all time is the 85–hour long *Cure For Insomnia* (1987).

The British film *Gandhi* (1982) used 300,000 extras during filming.

The character Sherlock Holmes has been portrayed by 75 actors in 211 films.

DATABANK

INPUT	OUTPUT
Q When did color films start to replace black and white?	**A** Color was first used in 1894, but only took over in the late 1960s.
Q What film won the most Academy Awards (Oscars)?	**A** *Ben-Hur* (1959) and *Titanic* (1997) both won 11 Oscars.
Q Which country's people go to the movies most often?	**A** Lebanese people go to the cinema over 35 times a year each!
Q What is regarded as the best movie of all time?	**A** Experts list *Citizen Kane* (1941); film buffs say *Casablanca* (1943).

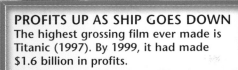

USE THE FORCE
The Empire Strikes Back (1980) was the second *Star Wars* film. The series is the most successful in movie history.

PROFITS UP AS SHIP GOES DOWN
The highest grossing film ever made is *Titanic* (1997). By 1999, it had made $1.6 billion in profits.

If inflation is taken into account, *Gone With the Wind* (1939) would be the highest-grossing film ever.

 ## Blockbusters

Hollywood's success since 1945 has rested partly on big budget films packed with stars. Using special effects, huge sets, and exotic locations, these movies are expensive, and not all of them make money. *Cutthroat Island* (1995) had losses of $80 million! One of the most successful series has been the *Indiana Jones* trilogy, starring Harrison Ford and directed by Steven Spielberg. Ford also starred in three *Star Wars* films. Other blockbusters include the *Batman* series and *Men in Black* (1997) starring Will Smith.

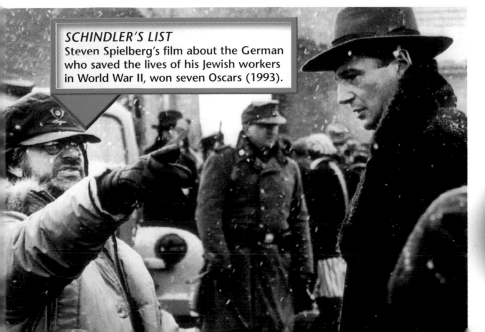

SCHINDLER'S LIST
Steven Spielberg's film about the German who saved the lives of his Jewish workers in World War II, won seven Oscars (1993).

Directors

Film direction is a highly regarded art. Alfred Hitchcock was an expert at creating suspense, while Stanley Kubrick was famous for his visual extravaganzas and attention to detail. Many actors, including Jodie Foster and Robert Redford, are also movie directors. Orson Welles managed to direct and star in *Citizen Kane* (1941). Tim Burton, who directed *Edward Scissorhands* (1990), is one of today's most popular directors.

FOOD AND DRINK

Food and drink are vital for existence—what we eat depends on factors such as religion or geographic location. Some rare foods have become luxury items.

 ## Farming

In developed countries, like the U.K. and U.S., machinery and large farms mean that agriculture is big business. In poorer areas, farming is small-scale, providing enough food for only the farmer's family. Cereals like wheat, maize, and rice are the most commonly grown foods, and make up half the world's food intake. Animal farming for meat, milk, wool, and leather is also vitally important. The world's most popular beverage is tea, made from a plant cultivated in China and India since 200 A.D. Coffee was first consumed in Ethiopia in the 1400s. As it became popular in Europe, the coffee plant was taken to Brazil and the Caribbean where it is now farmed on a massive scale.

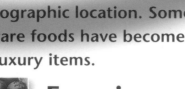

PADDY FIELDS
Rice is the main crop of countries such as China and India. It is grown in flooded fields to take advantage of seasonal rain.

In the U.S., farming employs only three percent of workers. Two hundred years ago, it was 90 percent.

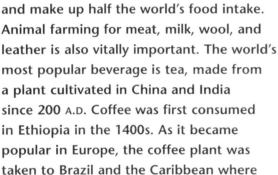

SWEET CROP
Sugar cane is the main source of sugar. It originates from Pacific islands. Sugar is also extracted from sugar beet.

BANANA REPUBLIC
Bananas are one of the most popular and nutritious tropical fruits. A single bunch can hold up to 150 bananas.

MECHANIZED FARMING
Machines such as the combine harvester make it easy for a handful of workers to farm an enormous area.

FACTS AND FIGURES

Across the world more people work in farming than in all other occupations combined.

In the U.S., each person eats about 60 pounds of chicken meat per year.

Instant coffee is strong liquid coffee that has been freeze-dried.

Saturated fat, found in meat and dairy foods, should only be 10 percent of an ideal diet.

The Australians are the biggest consumers of meat per person.

A cake preserved in an Egyptian tomb is thought to be about 4,200 years old.

Wild ginseng, a rare spice found in China, sells for up to $500,000 per gram.

What We Eat

A balanced diet provides us with energy for our activities and with the material our body needs to grow and repair itself. Different cultures have distinctive diets. Developed nations eat more meat than is healthy, while in India Hindus view animals as sacred, so they eat only vegetables. A Mediterranean diet centers on fresh seafood, fruit, and vegetables while Asian food is often spicy.

SHARK'S FIN
Shark's fin soup is so popular in many Asian countries that sharks may become extinct.

HAMBURGER
A popular food item in the U.S., the hamburger was introduced by German immigrants in the 1800s.

SPICE SALE
Spices play a vital part in Eastern cooking. Rare spices, such as saffron and wild ginseng, are very expensive.

Strange Tastes

Food and drink are basic requirements for life, but some have acquired a mystique because of their rarity and flavor, so they are expensive. These include Kopi Luwak, an Indonesian coffee. The beans are collected from the droppings of palm civets—a cat-size mammal—before being roasted. The civet's digestive system seems to give the coffee extra flavor. In Spain, fishermen brave storms to catch a rare barnacle. In Thailand and parts of southeast Asia, people risk their lives to collect swift nests from sea caves. Constructed from the bird's saliva, the nests are prized by chefs who make soup from them. Nests are advertised on the Internet for $1,000–$6,000 per pound.

TRUFFLES
Truffles are a type of rare fungus. They are expensive because they are difficult to find and cannot be grown. A white species from Italy sells for over $9,090 per lb.

CHOCOLATE
When chocolate first reached Europe from Mexico in the 1600s, only the wealthy could afford it.

A GOOD YEAR
The most expensive bottle of wine was a Château Lafite from 1787. It sold in 1985 for over $170,000.

EGG BOXES
Caviar, the eggs of the sturgeon fish, comes from Russia. The rarest type costs over $1,000 for 50g.

Truffle hunters in Europe use specially trained dogs or even pigs to find the precious fungus.

THE FUTURE

The last 1,000 years have seen many changes in the way we live, particularly the last few decades. The future looks exciting—but only if we are prepared to take care of our world.

ELECTRIC CAR
To cope with an increasing population, future transit may be cleaner and more efficient.

TAKING OVER
Robots are becoming more intelligent. An American robot is being developed that can hear, speak, feel, and think!

 ## Home Comforts

Houses with Internet connections in every room can be built, enabling people to operate appliances from far away. Computers can be programmed to water your garden while you are on vacation. Houses may be fitted with devices like "intelligent" smoke alarms. These can turn off gas or electricity if a problem is detected.

Scientists are able to clone animals. Many people are worried about the prospect of cloning humans.

 ## Genetics

By manipulating genes, scientists can alter animals and plants for our benefit. Some scientists would like to experiment on humans to combat disease and even remove unpleasant character traits. It may soon be possible to clone human organs so that each person may have spare organs stored for future transplants.

WIND FARM
Extraordinary sights, such as this wind farm, may one day become common in the quest for new power.

 ## Power

Electricity may become the chief power of the future. Today it is produced by burning coal, oil, or gas in power plants, yet reserves of oil are expected to run out by 2030 and coal by 2200. Nuclear power is also used by many countries, but it is not the safest option. Most experts think wind, tidal, or solar power will be used in the future.

NANOROBOTS
Scientists are currently developing machines small enough to travel through the bloodstream and repair any damage.

EARTHLINGS IN SPACE
Space cities may be placed in earth's orbit, providing bases for space ships and laboratories for scientists.

New Homes

The new millennium could witness a permanent human settlement on the moon. It would become a scientific research base and provide living space for thousands of people. The moon may also be a valuable stepping stone for missions to Mars. A few experts believe that the red planet could be turned into a new earth.

FACTS AND FIGURES

Machines that identify people by scanning their eyes will be common by 2010.

By 2010, most houses will have robots—they may even do all the housework.

Cash may soon be replaced with safe and easy to carry "smart" cards.

By the year 2030, robots may outnumber humans in developed countries.

Some experts believe that nanorobots will be in use by the year 2015.

LIFE ON MARS
A Mars mission may take place by 2030. The journey will take up to a year, so, after creating a base, the astronauts will need to process fuel from the planet for their return journey.

The End?

Since the invention of atom bombs, we have become aware of how easy it is to destroy life on earth. Global warming may melt the ice caps, turning the planet into a big ocean. Pollution could poison the land so that we cannot grow any food. Yet many experts believe that we will colonize other planets—and create new worlds.

SPLAT!
Space contains millions of huge asteroids, and many have hit earth in the past. Should one strike earth in the near future we could be wiped out, just as the dinosaurs were.

GLOSSARY

This section explains some of the more unusual or difficult terms that have been used in this book. The entries are arranged in alphabetical order.

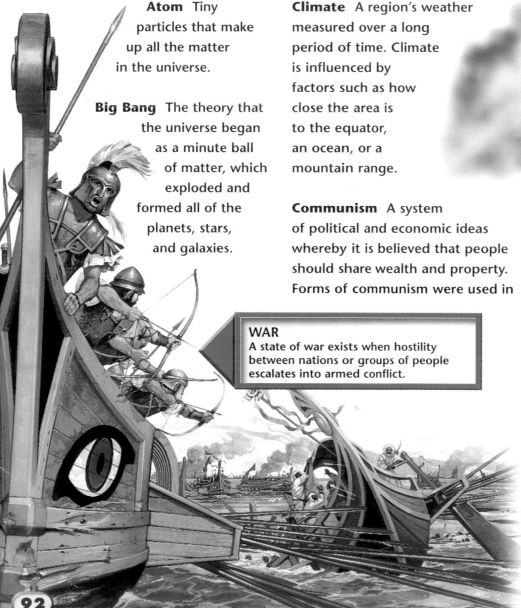

FORCE
The shuttle's rockets provide a thrusting force that enables it to escape the pulling force of earth's gravity.

Astrology The art of telling the future using the positions and movements of planets and stars; the belief these have an influence on human affairs.

Astronomy The scientific study of space and everything within it.

Atom Tiny particles that make up all the matter in the universe.

Big Bang The theory that the universe began as a minute ball of matter, which exploded and formed all of the planets, stars, and galaxies.

Black hole When a large star uses up all its fuel, it can collapse in upon itself, creating a black hole. A black hole has a huge gravitational pull and attracts all other objects, including light, toward it.

Climate A region's weather measured over a long period of time. Climate is influenced by factors such as how close the area is to the equator, an ocean, or a mountain range.

Communism A system of political and economic ideas whereby it is believed that people should share wealth and property. Forms of communism were used in the former Soviet Union (Russia and its republics) and eastern Europe until the early 1990s. It survives in China and Cuba.

Developed countries This term is used to describe the wealthy, industrial nations of the world. These include the U.S., Japan, and western European countries.

Eclipse This occurs when a planet or moon moves into the shadow of another. On earth, a solar eclipse occurs when the moon's shadow falls on part of earth, creating a period of darkness during the day.

Element An element, such as oxygen, gold, or carbon, is a basic substance that cannot be broken down into other substances. Each contains just one type of atom.

WAR
A state of war exists when hostility between nations or groups of people escalates into armed conflict.

Environment Earth and everything within in it, including plants, animals, people, air, and the soil. Our destruction of parts of the environment threatens earth's future.

Fascism The belief that the state is more important than its citizens. Fascism took hold in parts of Europe, particularly in Italy and Germany. Adolf Hitler's Nazi party was Fascist. They gained and held power in Germany using violence and intimidation.

Fossil Remains of an animal or plant preserved in rock. Over long periods of time, a fossil becomes part of the rock itself or just an impression in rock.

Galaxy A group of stars held together by their own gravity. There are thought to be billions of galaxies in the universe, each containing millions of stars. The earth's galaxy is called the Milky Way.

Genetics The study of why living things look and behave as they do. Genes are the molecules within the body that carry the information to make a new organism look and behave as it does.

Gravity A force of attraction between objects. The larger the object and the closer you are to it, the greater the force you feel. For example, earth exerts a strong pull on everything on its surface.

Invertebrate Any animal that does not have a backbone. Includes insects, arachnids, crustaceans, worms, mollusks, and jellyfish.

Middle Ages An era of history—also known as the medieval period—that began with the fall of the Roman Empire in about A.D. 400 and ended in about A.D. 1450–80.

Millennium A period of one thousand years.

Nuclear reaction By splitting atoms, scientists release a vast amount of energy. This nuclear power is used to produce electricity and is the basis for atom bombs.

Organism Any living thing, including all plants and animals.

Prehistoric A term referring to the history of the world before humans began making written records (about 3000 B.C.).

Religion The belief in God or gods—who are usually entitled to obedience and worship. Major religions include Buddhism, Christianity, Islam, and Judaism.

Renaissance A movement in art, literature, and science that took place from about 1350 to 1550 based on a revival of ancient learning. It began in Italy.

Revolution The overthrow of a government by its subjects. Revolutions have occurred in many countries including France (1789), Russia (1917), and the U.S. (1775).

Universe Encompasses everything that exists—from the largest galaxy in space to the tiniest atom particle on a pinhead. The universe is unimaginably large.

Vertebrate Any animal with a backbone, such as fish, amphibians, reptiles, birds, and mammals.

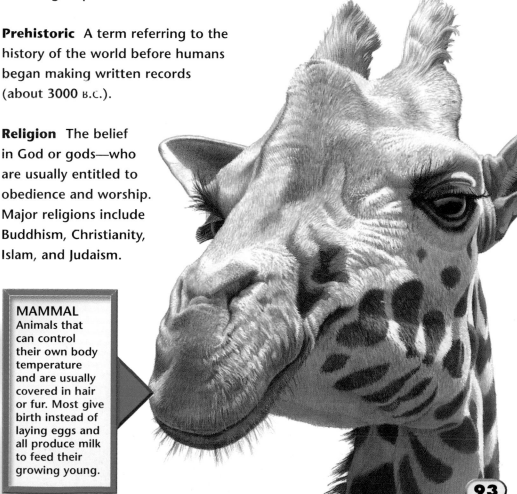

MAMMAL
Animals that can control their own body temperature and are usually covered in hair or fur. Most give birth instead of laying eggs and all produce milk to feed their growing young.

INDEX

ACKNOWLEDGMENTS

The publishers would like to thank the following:

 ## Photographs

Page 17-18 Tony Stone Images; 19(tr) Tony Stone Images/David Woodfall; 40(b) Popperfoto; 41(bl) Popperfoto; 48(bl) Mary Evans Picture Library; 49(tl) Mary Evans Picture Library; 50(tl) Popperfoto/Mike Blake/Reuters, (bc) Popperfoto/Dave Joiner, (br & bl) Popperfoto; 51(tl) Popperfoto/Brunskill, (cc) Popperfoto/Kimimasa Mayama/Reuters, (br) Popperfoto/Wolfgang/Reuters; 52-53(tr/tl) Popperfoto/Ray Stubblebine/Reuters; 53(tr) Popperfoto, (br) Popperfoto/Mike Blake/Reuters; 54(c & br) Popperfoto/Dave Joiner; 55(cr) Popperfoto/Monte Fresco; 56(bl) Popperfoto/Dave Joiner; 56–57(tr/tl) Popperfoto; 57(tc) Popperfoto, (cr) Popperfoto/David Joiner, (bl) Popperfoto/Bob Thomas Sports Photography; 58(tr) Science Photo Library/Ken Eward; p64(cl) Tony Stone Images, (bl) Science Photo Library/NOAA, coloured by John Wells, (bcl) Science Photo Library/NRSC Ltd., (bcr) Science Photo Library/Massonnet et al/CNES, (br) Planet Earth Pictures; 77(tl) Popperfoto/David Loh/Reuters, (c & br) Popperfoto; 79 The Stock Market; 80(b) Bridgeman Art Library/Vatican Museums and Galleries, Vatican; 80/81(tr/tl) Bridgeman Art Library/Art Institute of Chicago; 81(br) Popperfoto/D Osborn/Reuters; 82-83 (r/l) Mary Evans Picture Library; 83(tr) Mary Evans Picture Library, (bl) The Kobal Collection; 84(bl) Mary Evans Picture Library; 84–85(tr/tl) Popperfoto/Kieran Doherty/Reuters; 85(tr) Popperfoto/Peter Morgan/Reuters, (cl) Popperfoto; 87(tr) Popperfoto/Merle W Wallace/Reuters, (cl) Lucas Films, (br) Popperfoto/Reuters; 89(br) Tony Stone Images, (bl) The Anthony Blake Photo Library; 90 (cl) Science Photo Library, (br) Julian Baum

65(tc) Electronic Arts, (bc) Yahoo! homepage courtesy of Yahoo! Inc
82 *Harry Potter & the Chamber of Secrets* by J.K. Rowling, published by Bloomsbury Publishing Plc in 1998. Cover illustration from artwork by Cliff Wright, 1998

The following images are all courtesy of *The Illustrated London News*: 8(tr), 37(br); 40(cl & br), 41(tl & r & bc & br), 52(tc & br), 54(tr & bl); 76(tl), 86(tr & c)

Key: b=bottom, c=center, l=left, r=right, t=top

 ## Artists & Contributors

Every effort has been made to credit the artists whose work appears in this book and the publishers apologize to those whose names do not appear below:

Susanna Addario; Marion Appleton; Ray Arinaway; Julian Baker; Julian Baum; Simone Boni; Peter Bull; Robin Carter; Jim Channel; Harry Clow; Tom Connell; Peter Dennis; David Farren; James Field; Chris Forsey; Luigi Galante; Jeremy Gower; John Hayson; Ron Hayward; Adam Hook; Christian Hook; Richard Hook; Mark Iley; Kuo Kang Chen; Ian Jackson; Bridgette James; Michael Johnson; Mike Lacey; Linden Artists; Bernard Long; Steinar Lund; Kevin Maddison; Maltings Partnership; Janos Marfy; Angus McBride; Stefan Morris; Steve Noon; Alex Pang; Darren Pattenden; Elizabeth Rice; Bernard Robinson; Michael Roffe; Mike Saunders; Claudia Saraceni; John Scorey; Sitna; Guy Smith; Mike Taylor; Ross Watton; David Webb; Wildlife Art Agency; Ann Winterbotham

Contributors
Fergus Collins, Robert Cave, Luke Hutson, Richard Emerson

Design
Mik Gates, Julia Smith

The publishers also wish to thank Guinness World Records Ltd.

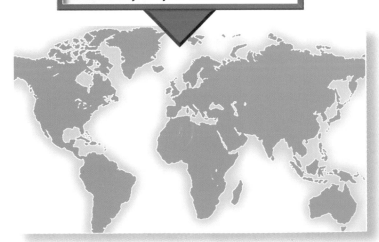

GETTING BIGGER ALL THE TIME
The population of the world is currently around 6 billion. It is projected to reach 14 billion by the year 2100.